Walk!

The Lake District North

with

Vivienne Crow

DISCOVERY WALKING GUIDES LTD

Walk! The Lake District North
First Edition - January 2006
Copyright © 2006

Published by
Discovery Walking Guides Ltd
10 Tennyson Close, Northampton NN5 7HJ,
England

Mapping supplied by **Global Mapping Limited**
(www.globalmapping.com)

Mapping sourced from | **o|s Ordnance Survey®** This product includes mapping data licensed from **Ordnance Survey®** with the permission of the Controller of Her Majesty's Stationery Office. © Crown Copyright 2005. All rights reserved.
Licence Number 40044851

Photographs
All photographs in this book are the property of the
author.
Front Cover Photographs

Loweswater (Walk 32)

**On Long Band
(Walk 10)**

**Looking down Pasture
Beck (Walk 8)**

**A frosty Scales Fell, as seen
from Blencathra (Walk 2)**

ISBN 1-904946-15-1
Text and photographs* © Vivienne Crow

Walk!

The Lake District North

CONTENTS

THE WALKS

B HELVELLYN & FAIRFIELD RANGES

C NORTHERN FELLS

THE AUTHOR

vienne has been a keen hill-walker since leaving her home town of London the age of 18. Having lived on the edge of the Peak District for several years, e had a brief spell in Northamptonshire until her longing for the hills forced r north again. She now lives in Cumbria, close to the Lake District.

journalist by trade, she gave up full-ne work a few years ago to go velling in Asia and New Zealand. nce her return, she has focused her ergies on the activities she loves most l-walking, writing, travelling and otography. As well as a weekly lking column in three newspapers in rth Cumbria, she writes vel/outdoors features for a variety of blications around the world and rks part-time as a sub-editor.

ACKNOWLEDGEMENTS

Ros and David for keeping me on the straight and narrow, Charles for eeping me informed and Heleyne for keeping me company.

INTRODUCTION

THE LAKE DISTRICT and THE FINE ART OF WALKING

The Lake District is to leisure walking what Vienna is to the waltz, Venice to canalization, Bletchley to code-breaking and Chicago to the blues. None of these places invented the related pursuit, but in each the activity was honed to a fine art.

The Romantic poets were drawn to the Lakes

Nowadays, our passion for wild places is so widespread it seems innate, but it only really evolved as a popular ideal in the eighteenth century, when a growing appreciation of the picturesque and the increasing security of the English countryside made walking in an undomesticated environment fashionable for the first time. And the place where this new fashion found its fullest expression was the Lake District.

With superb lakes carved into spectacularly sculpted valleys, long rugged ridges blessed with imposing panoramas, jagged crags dangling from grand peaks, sweeping dales cradling remote hamlets, and barren fells tonsured with ancient settlements, the Lake District had everything the dedicated wilderness seeker could desire.

The summit of Helvellyn

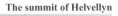

It was this 'wilderness' that attracted poets such as Thomas Gray, who published the first book about the region in 1775, Coleridge, who made the first recorded ascent of England's highest summit (**Scafell Pike**) in 1802, and of course Wordsworth, who is said to have clocked up some 180,000 pedestrian miles, in the course of which he helped transform walking from an irksome necessity into an enviable indulgence.

For Wordsworth, walking was literally poetry in motion, most of his poems being composed as he walked, but it was also a means of escaping the social and political constraints of his age.

Anyone who has since walked to get away from the clatter and clutter of the workaday world is following in his footsteps.

Some of the trails the Romantic poets enjoyed are now under asphalt, others are so heavily used their charm is marred, but the grandeur and beauty of the landscape are undiminished, and it's still possible to hike in isolation on seemingly untamed land amid vistas that would wring a poem from the most prosaic spectator.

From Robinson

So if you think walking is more than a means of getting from A to B, if you like using your body to traverse terrain that is breathtaking in more than a merely respiratory sense, if you want to wash your mind of the commonplace cares that accumulate in the course of everyday living, if you want a world that's a little wider than the one you normally encounter… if, in short, you enjoy the fine art of walking, the Lake District is the place for you.

ON THE PAGE: USING THE BOOK

The Lake District is essentially a massive volcanic dome fissured by tectonic pressure and then sculpted by glaciation to create a spray of valleys and dividing ridges radiating from a central hub like the spokes of a wheel. There are eleven valleys, sixteen lakes and 315 'mountains', 170 of them over 2,000ft (610m, the defining height for a mountain in the Encyclopaedia Britannica), four over 3000ft (914m, the only four of this height in England). The aim of this book is to provide an outline for a preliminary exploration of the major summits, ridges and valleys in the northern half of the area.

On Dollywaggon Pike

The walks, none of which is more than a 30-minute drive from **Keswick**, are divided into six geographical areas: the eastern fells, the **Helvellyn** and **Fairfield** ranges, the **Northern Fells**, walks above **Borrowdale**, the north-western fells and the western fells.

For each area I've included some of the classics, plus a selection of less celebrated and therefore less crowded itineraries. On some of the longer routes, I've suggested escape routes that can be used in emergencies or if the weather suddenly turns bad.

Within each section, the walks are featured in ascending order of difficulty, the first being an easy excursion suitable as a test walk or in bad weather, the last a longer, more challenging itinerary.

To help assess the nature of a walk, each itinerary is prefaced by a brief introduction and a rating guide detailing exertion, walking time, distance, ascents and descents, refreshments and access.

Each walk includes information on distance

Timings are all 'pure' timings excluding the rich variety of distraction and lethargy that can extend the simplest walk almost indefinitely. If you are ticking off Wainwrights against the clock, you will doubtless regard my timings with disdain, but everyone else should allow at least 15 minutes more per walking hour for snacking, snapping and standing still staring. There's nothing more frustrating than trying to walk at someone else's speed, be it faster or slower than your own - so take *your* time and ignore mine if it doesn't match.

Exertion ratings are subjective. Do an easy walk first then judge the rest accordingly.

Hopefully, refreshment ratings are more objective, but there's no accounting for taste, so bear in mind that my criteria may not match your own.

ON THE GROUND: MAN AND THE LANDSCAPE

The Lake District mountains are among the oldest in the world, the youngest rocks being more than 200 million years old. Limestone and red sandstone can be found at the park boundaries, but the bulk of the area can be divided into three rock types – the Skiddaw Slates, the Borrowdale Volcanic Series and the Silurian Slates.

Laid down by sedimentary processes more than 450 million years ago, the Skiddaw Slates in the north of Lake District are the oldest rocks. Hardened and compressed on the sea bed, they tend to give us steep, smooth, rounded fells. The rough, angular landscape of the central fells is attributed to the Borrowdale Volcanic Series, made up of lava and ash that has been hardened. Further south, the smaller fells are made up of Silurian Slates, similar to the rocks of northern Lakeland, but much younger.

Much of the landscape that we see today was sculpted by the Ice Ages. The advance of the glaciers gouged out deep valleys and created *arêtes*, waterfalls in hanging valleys and long, narrow lakes held back by terminal *moraine* – a pile of clay and stone abandoned by the retreating ice. High in the mountains, the ice plucked out *corries*, which are now home to tarns.

Blea Water on High Street is a glacial feature

Like any rugged landscape, the mountains which encompass the Lake District were a barrier to human incursion, but it's a long time since the region was really a wilderness. Even when civilization was at its most rudimentary, these mountains were worked and shaped by man, and the 'wildness' we enjoy today is heavily compromised.

The wealth of different rock types gave rise to rich mining and quarrying industries. The Romans were the first to notice the potential, mining for copper on **Coniston Old Man**, but it wasn't until the sixteenth and seventeenth centuries that the industry really took off.

The former mining village of Hartsop

Today, it's hard to escape the mining legacy - the Lake District is dotted with ruined or renovated mine buildings, spoil heaps, scarred mountainsides, disused dams and the leats used to transport water around the fells.

The forests were cleared as grazing land for the sheep that were vital to medieval England's wealth, or cut back for ships' timbers, bobbins for textile mills and fuel for smelting.

This clear land is laced with a web of trails and ways, including Roman roads, peat roads, 'corpse' or 'coffin' roads connecting hamlets to consecrated graveyards, sheep tracks, drovers' and packmen's trails and mining paths.

Forests were cleared for sheep

Had man not intervened, the mountains would be mantled in a cloak of oak, birch and pine above which only the highest peaks would be visible, and the valleys would be impenetrable swamps picketed with alder and dense sedges.

Instead, we have expansive moor and pasture, partitioned by dry-stone walling and sprinkled with well-defined lakes and reservoirs.

Nowadays, patches of sessile oak remain on dry ground, while the damp is dotted with stands of birch and alder. There are also holly, cherry, crabapple, rowan, witch-hazel and yew, but the most common trees are the conifers, grimly regimented in the last century when reverence for the picturesque yielded to more pressing economic imperatives.

Recent years have seen some attempts to rid the landscape of the some of the miserable conifer plantations as in **Ennerdale**, where a partnership of the National Trust, The Forestry Commission and United Utilities is felling the spruce trees planted in the 1920s in the hope that native broad-leaf trees will return.

Holme Woods beside Loweswater

Wildflowers are limited, but one can see wood anemone, asphodels, red campion, lady's mantle, bog myrtle, spotted orchids, saxifrage, stonecrop, saw-worth and thrift - and, of course, the odd daffodil. The most varied plants are heather, lichen and moss.

Despite centuries of human interference, the Lake District remains relatively rich in birdlife. The fell-tops are home all year round to ravens, buzzards, peregrines and, in the eastern fells, England's last surviving golden eagle. Spring migrants include the wheatear and ring ouzel (mountain blackbird). Lower down, in the spring, you'll encounter a range of migratory species, including redstart, pied flycatcher, wood warbler and tree pipit among the year-round residents such as chaffinch, green and great-spotted woodpeckers, nuthatch and sparrowhawk. On the lakes themselves, you can find good numbers of waterfowl, goosander, goldeneye and tufted duck, while rivers and streams are home to dippers, grey wagtails and common sandpipers. A pair of ospreys have recently made the Lake District their summer home, returning from wintering in Africa to their nest in **Wythop Woods** on the shores of **Bassenthwaite Lake** every April.

High fell fauna include foxes, hares and stoats. Herds of red deer can also be seen above the tree line, especially in the **Martindale** area of the eastern Lake District and on the **Furness Fells**. The woods are home to badgers, roe deer, voles, shrews, the occasional otter and, of course, red squirrels.

Another way of approaching the history of a landscape is through toponymy. Looking at a map of the Lake District, you will see a pattern of affixes and root words, suggesting a landscape defined by language long before the Romantics began waxing lyrical.

Place names ending with -ton, -ham, -ington indicate a seventh century Anglian community. Scandinavian settlements from the ninth and tenth centuries carry suffixes such as -beck, -booth, -fell, -gill, -slack, and -thwaite, while Norse words are also at the root of **Greta** (Coleridge's Keswick residence - *griot à* a rocky or gravelly river), **Ullswater** (Ulf's Lake) and **Ambleside** (Hamel's Saetre or farm).

I wandered lonely as a cloud...

It's a grand line of poetry, economically evoking one of the great pleasures of walking, but as a piece of reportage, it's pretty flabby stuff. Either that or Wordsworth was a strikingly convivial hiker, because if there's one thing clouds aren't in the Lake District, it's lonely. Great gregarious gangs of the things come gambolling in from the Irish Sea, and any cloud looking for solitude would have to be very quick off the mark indeed.

Yes, **Borrowdale** *is* the wettest place in England, but that doesn't mean that you're always going to get a good soaking in the Lake District. With the prevailing weather coming in rapidly from the south-west, conditions can change quickly. One of the great joys of the region is its ever-changing skies - you can sit atop a fell, black storm clouds to the east, watching skittery showers passing just a few hundred yards to the north, while bathed in warm rays breaking through the white lumps above. Boring it ain't!

Yes! You might get your boots wet!

If you're properly equipped, the climate need not be a problem. The most vital piece of equipment is information. Always phone the recorded forecast (0870 0550575) before setting out for the high fells and opt for a low-level walk if bad weather is imminent. In the winter, this forecast also includes an assessment of the fell-top conditions - including depth, condition and likely locations of snow and ice - that is updated daily.

Clouds descend on Great Gable

This is always a slightly dreary section of a book rehearsing the dos-and-don'ts, but even for experienced walkers, it's worth reminding yourself that a mountain outing can be made miserable or dangerous by lack of planning.

A few of the itineraries in this book cover short sections that many walkers would describe as scrambles. Technical scramblers, on the other hand, would

Striding Edge

beg to differ. If I describe a section as a "scramble", I simply mean that you will need your hands as you clamber up or down the rocks. There are no technical scrambles in *Walk! The Lake District North*.

Likewise, the term "vertiginous" is relative. Some people may find the flat, broad top of **Skiddaw** vertiginous, although I haven't yet met any who do! When I describe a route as possibly vertiginous, I mean there may be one or two sections of narrow ridge with steep drops on either side. It's best to read the description in advance, so you know what manner of walk you're taking on.

Equipment is equally important to a pleasurable outing. Coleridge used to set off for a three-day walking tour wearing a great coat and carrying a spare pair of socks in his pocket, but he didn't have the many outdoor gear shops of **Keswick** and **Ambleside** at his disposal.

Even in the height of summer, your daysack should contain the wherewithal to make yourself wind and waterproof. Most people will carry several layers of clothing as well as wind and waterproof layers. As far as boots go, I'm a little old-fashioned myself - I like a good, solid leather boot with plenty of ankle support when I'm heading for the high fells. Others prefer something lighter.

Pillar from Hay Stacks

Whatever you wear, make sure it has a good grip and isn't likely to result in a twisted ankle on uneven ground. If it's waterproof too, that's a bonus. If not, think about investing in some gaiters. There's nothing more disappointing than getting your boots so totally drenched in heavy rain one day that you're unable to take advantage of the next day's brilliant sunshine.

Every walker needs to carry a map and compass - and know how to use them. See also the section on using GPS on page 21. Always take basic rations, even if you don't intend picnicking. Emergency equipment should at least include a whistle and a torch - the distress signal being six flashes/whistle-blasts repeated at one-minute intervals. Some fellwalkers suggest carrying a bin bag or space blanket in case you have to stay out overnight; many carry small first aid kits. Remember that a mobile phone is not an adequate substitute for basic safety precautions - especially as reception can be intermittent at best in some areas of the Lake District.

Though often ignored, the basic rule, "Tell someone where you're going", has to be repeated. The unspoken rider is, "Phone that someone if there's a change of plan". Rescue parties do not delight in the news that the 'missing' walker they've been searching for on windswept fells was actually lost in a pint down the pub.

Stick to the Countryside Code. The main change in the new code, revised in 2004, brings theory into line with sensible practice, changing the old rule about always shutting gates to leaving them as you found them.

Leave gates as you find them

ON THE ROAD: GETTING THERE AND GETTING ABOUT

Driving in the Lake District can be delightful or dismal, depending on how many other people are doing it at the same time as you. On weekdays out of season, private transport is the most versatile way of getting around, but in summer and on Bank Holiday weekends a car can be a liability.

For a full guide to national and local public transport, see www.traveline.org.uk. Also see the Appendices at the back of this book. You can also telephone Traveline (0870 608 2608), but if you're calling from a fixed line, dial 141 first to avoid being put through to your local information centre as opposed to the Cumbria centre. The best place to stay if you're relying on public transport is probably **Keswick**.

The nearest mainline train stations to the North Lakes are **Penrith, Carlisle** and **Oxenholme**. A branch line follows the coast from **Barrow** in the south right round to **Carlisle** in the north, stopping at **Whitehaven, Workington, Maryport** and **Wigton** among others. There is also a short line from **Oxenholme** to **Windermere**.

National Express buses (www.nationalexpressgroup.com) connect north Cumbria with destinations throughout the UK.

Day-trippers may wish to consider a public transport day pass, available from local service providers and tourist offices. There are various options combining train, bus and boat.

And finally…

On the high fells

During my love affair with the Lake District, which includes writing a weekly walking column for three local newspapers, I have trodden each of the paths described in this book several times. But things change - stiles become gates, woodland gets ripped up, cairns get knocked down and footpaths get diverted. Just bear this in mind and don't curse my name too loudly on the fells when not all goes according to plan.

3 our rating for effort/exertion:-
1 very easy **2** easy **3** average
4 energetic **5** strenuous

 approximate **time** to complete
a walk (compare your times
against ours early in a walk) -
does not include stopping time

 5 miles/8km approximate walking **distance** in miles/kilometres

 approximate **ascents/descents** in metres (N=negligible)

 circular route

 linear route

 figure of eight route

 risk of **vertigo**

 refreshments (may be at start or end of a route only)

Walk descriptions include:
- timing in minutes, shown as (40M)
- compass directions, shown as (NW)
- heights in metres, shown as (1355m)
- GPS waypoints, shown as (Wp.3)

Notes on the text
Place names are shown in **bold text**, except where we refer to a written sign, when they are enclosed in single quotation marks. Local or unusual words are shown in *italics*, and are explained in the accompanying text.

ORDNANCE SURVEY MAPPING

All the map sections which accompany the detailed walk descriptions in Walk! The Lake District North are reproduced under Ordnance Survey licence from the digital versions of the latest Explorer 1:25,000 scale maps. Each map section is then re-scaled to the 40,000 scale used in DWG's Walk!/Walks series of guide books. Walking Route and GPS Waypoints are then drawn onto the map section to produce the map illustrating the detailed walk description.

Walk! Lake District North map sections are sufficient for following the detailed walk descriptions, but for planning your adventures in this region, and if you to divert from the walking routes, we strongly recommend that you purchase the latest OS Explorer maps.

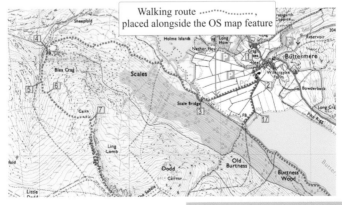

Walking route ....,
placed alongside the OS map feature

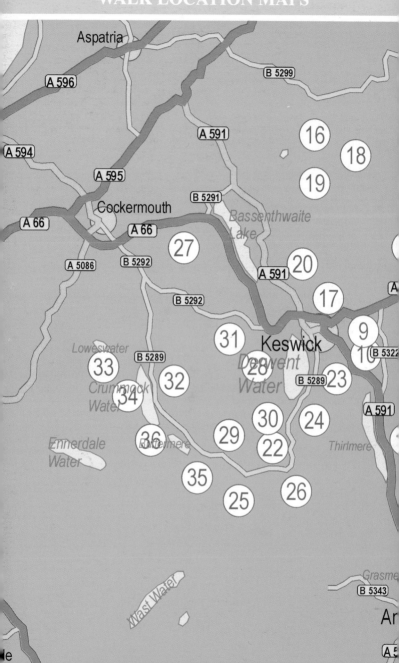

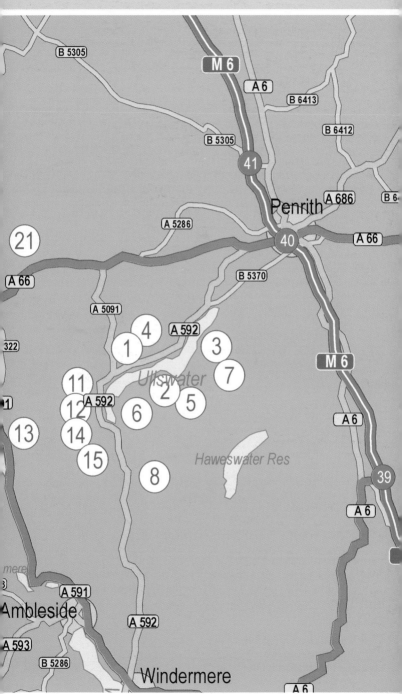

The GPS Waypoint lists provided in this book are as recorded by Vivienne Crow while researching the detailed walk descriptions. Waypoint symbols are numbered so that they can be directly identified with the walk description and waypoint list. All GPS Waypoints are subject to the accuracy of GPS units in the particular location of each waypoint.

In the dramatic landscapes of the Lake District, GPS reception is surprisingly good for the majority of Vivienne's walking routes. Only her first walk, Aira Force, defies the use of GPS navigation.

Satellite Reception
Accurate location fixes for your GPS unit depend upon you receiving signals from four or more satellites. Providing you have good batteries, and that you wait until your GPS has full 'satellite acquisition' before starting out, your GPS will perform well in the Lake District. Where Vivienne has encountered poor satellite reception it is mentioned in the walk description.

Manually Inputting Waypoints
GPS Waypoints are quoted for the OSGB (Ordnance Survey Great Britain) datum and BNG (British National Grid) coordinates, making them identical with the OS grid coordinates of the position they refer to. To manually input the Waypoints into your GPSs we suggest that you:

- switch on your GPS and select 'simulator/standby' mode
- check that your gps is set to the OSGB datum and BNG 'location/position format'
- input the GPS Waypoints into a 'route' with the same number as the walking route; then when you call up the 'route' in the Lake District there will be no confusion as to which walking route it refers
- repeat the inputting of waypoints into routes until you have covered all the routes you plan to walk, or until you have used up the memory capacity of your GPS
- turn off your GPS. When you turn your GPS back on it should return to its normal navigation mode
- note that GPS Waypoints complement the routes in Walk! The Lake District North, and are not intended as an alternative to the detailed walking route descriptions

Personal Navigator Files (PNFs) CD version 3.01
Edited versions of Vivienne's original GPS research tracks and waypoints are available as downloadable files on our PNFs CD; which also includes all the edited GPS tracks and waypoints for all the Walk!/Walks guide books published by DWG along with GPS Utility Special edition software. See DWG websites for more information

www.walking.demon.co.uk & www.dwgwalking.co.uk

GPS The Easy Way (£4.99)
If you are confused by talk of GPS, but are interested in how this modern navigational aid could enhance your walking enjoyment, then simply seek out a copy of GPS The Easy Way, the UK's best selling GPS manual.

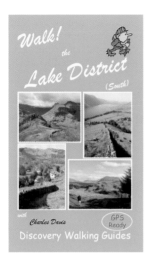

If you enjoy this book, then try its companion volume, **Walk! The Lake District South**. The author, Charles Davis, is an experienced walking book researcher and author with a fistful of titles to his name.

Walk! The Lake District South
with Charles Davis
published by
Discovery Walking Guides Ltd.
ISBN 1-904946-16-X

For a full list of Discovery Walking Guides publications, see our websites:
www.walking.demon.co.uk and www.dwgwalking.co.uk

or write to:
Discovery Walking Guides Ltd.
10 Tennyson Close
Northampton (England)
NN5 7HJ

Walk! Wire-O Spiral Bound Guidebooks are designed to be used with:

- DWG's plastic slipcover (PSC), which prevents the binding from catching on pockets and increases durability -
- - and our clear plastic All Weather Book Bag (AWBB) with grip-top seal which allows the book to be folded back displaying 2 pages, then sealed, impervious to weather conditions.

To obtain your PSC and AWBB for this book, send a C5 (9 x 7 inch) SAE with 47p stamp, to:
(Code 9781904946151)
Discovery Walking Guides
10 Tennyson Close
Northampton NN5 7HJ

This gentle introduction to the Lake District visits one of the area's most impressive waterfalls and a nineteenth century arboretum. (GPS reception is poor throughout the **Aira Force** gorge.)

Access by car: The walk starts at the National Trust car park beside **Aira Force** (GR NY400200) at the junction of the A5091 and A592, 13 miles SE of **Keswick**.

Access by bus: Aira Force is served all year round by bus Nº108 from **Penrith** to **Patterdale** and, in the summer, by bus Nº208, **Keswick** to **Patterdale** (see appendix).

Like the gateway in 'The Secret Garden', the gap in the National Trust stone construction at the far end of the car park (Wp.1 0M) holds the key to a number of surprises. Going through, we follow the path along the woodland edge and then through a gap in a drystone wall (3M). Bearing right to briefly follow some iron railings on our right, we go through a gap in the railings to cross pretty **Aira Beck** via a footbridge.

Trudging up the stone staircase on the other side, we bear left at the fork at the top (Wp.2 8M), passing close to two magnificent sitka spruces. A much maligned species due to over-planting in British plantations, this pair was planted in 1846. The largest has a girth of more than six metres (20 feet), placing it in the top seven largest sitka spruces in the UK.

Aira Force

Ignoring another steep stairway off to the right, we reach and cross a stone bridge at the base of the falls (Wp.3 13M), delighting in the spray as the beck plummets noisily through the gorge.

It won't come as a surprise to discover that Wordsworth was a frequent visitor to the area, and was inspired to write three poems about **Aira Force**, the most well known being 'The Somnambulist'. Having taken our photos, we climb the steep staircase on the other side of the gorge and turn right at the top.

Still puffing and panting from that last climb, we continue following the tumbling beck upstream, ignoring the humpback stone bridge to the right. We only re-cross when we reach a small, wooden footbridge (Wp.4 21M) that crosses a particularly narrow, steep-sided section of gorge.

Turning right on the other side, we plod up yet another steep, stony staircase to begin our return route with the beck now on our right.

The humpback bridge over Aira Force

We join a path coming in from the left and, 50 yards later, bear right at a fork to plummet back down to the water's edge.

Having crossed the humpback bridge that we saw earlier (Wp.5 30M), we ascend the few steps on the opposite side of the beck and then bear left to head downstream with the beck on our left.

The woodland here contains a number of wonderful specimens, including a Douglas fir, which is the tallest tree in Cumbria, some fine yews and a Chilean pine or 'Monkey Puzzle' tree. Many of the trees were planted by the Howard family of **Greystoke**, lords of the manor here from the late Middle Ages until they sold the land to the National Trust in 1906.

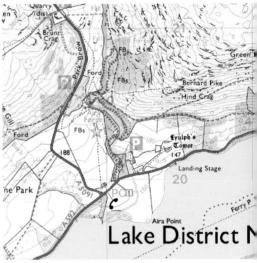

Reaching the iron railings that we walked beside at the beginning of the walk (Wp.6), we bear right and stroll through the woods back to the car park.

This is a great little winter walk, ideal for short days or when snow makes the high fells just a bit too much of a challenge. It's also good for a summer's morning, when the sun is glinting brilliantly off serene **Ullswater**.

The lakeshore path is quite popular, but the western side of **Hallin Fell** sometimes feels quite remote. The route entails an easy stroll around the base of the fell and along the shores of **Ullswater**, a short climb up on to **Hallin Fell** (388 metres) for some wonderful views across the lake and an optional extension to **St Martin's Church**.

The climb on to the top can easily be avoided by turning right instead of left at Wp.7 to make a grade 1 walk. Alternatively, to upgrade the excursion, the route can be added to Walk 5 (Pikeawassa) for a figure-of-eight walk and a much longer day out.

*   - or 3.7 miles without the church extension

**   Though not on the walking route, **Pooley Bridge** (as you drive back to civilisation) offers pub refreshment.

Access by car: you'll need to drive to the start of the walk, which is **St Peter's Church** in **Martindale** (GR NY435191), 4.4 miles SW of **Pooley Bridge**.

From the parking area (Wp.1 0M), we walk along the road towards **Pooley Bridge**, bearing left along a grassy path just 120 yards beyond the church (Wp.2 1M). Staying parallel with the road for a short while, we soon swing away from it to catch our first glimpse of beautiful **Ullswater**. Passing a kissing-gate on our right (10M), we swing round to the left as we circle the base of **Hallin Fell**.

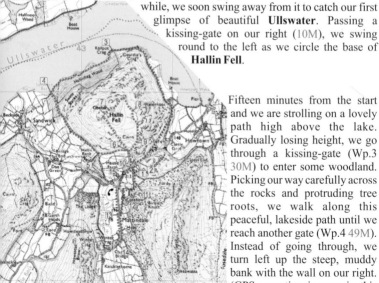

Fifteen minutes from the start and we are strolling on a lovely path high above the lake. Gradually losing height, we go through a kissing-gate (Wp.3 30M) to enter some woodland. Picking our way carefully across the rocks and protruding tree roots, we walk along this peaceful, lakeside path until we reach another gate (Wp.4 49M). Instead of going through, we turn left up the steep, muddy bank with the wall on our right. (GPS reception is poor in this area of the woods.)

Struggling upwards, we go through another gate (54M) to leave the woods. The gradient eases as we make our way to a level section of path where we are greeted by a glorious vista of smooth, grassy fells and verdant valleys. The fell to our right, just appearing from behind the trees, is **Place Fell**, and to its south is **Beda Fell** (see Walk 6 for a circuit of the two). The next valley over is **Martindale**, where we'll be heading later to see the old church, and to its left is **Steel Knotts** and **Pikeawassa** (see Walk 5).

We leave the wall at a faint fork in the path (Wp.5 65M) to bear left along the clearer path, heading slightly uphill. The path soon levels off as we are joined by another wall to our right, then part company with it at the next corner (Wp.6 70M). As the wall turns sharp right, we turn left to be greeted by a multitude of green swathes heading up the fell; we take the rising path furthest left (NW).

On Hallin Fell

Climbing easily on the short turf, we soon reach the surprisingly large nineteenth century obelisk that marks the summit of this little fell (Wp.7 84M) - an excuse to get the picnic out and relax while enjoying those stunning views down **Ullswater**.

Coming away from the top (ENE), we drop into a dip. Ignoring a faint path off to the right, we start losing height more rapidly as we shoot down the north-eastern side of the fell, our eyes inevitably drawn to the expanse of dark blue water straight ahead of us. No wonder Wordsworth was so inspired by **Ullswater**!

At the bottom of this initial descent we swing right, then bear right at a fork (Wp.8 94M). There's a multitude of paths criss-crossing the fell and you're unlikely to get lost whichever one you pick - **Hallin Fell** stands isolated from all its neighbours, so the worst that can happen is that you'll end up wandering round in circles for a while. (A real possibility in mist!)

At a dip between two small hillocks, we are joined by a path coming in from the left as we descend towards lonely **Martindale**. Ignoring the faint track off to the left when we reach a prominent cairn (Wp.9 103M), we choose the right-hand path. Always sticking with the clearest option ahead, we thunder down the slope and back to the corner of the wall at Wp.7. Now, we turn left to reach the road opposite **St Peter's Church** (Wp.10

Looking towards Beda Fell

109M).

You can end the walk here if you want, but you'd miss out on the lovely stroll into **Martindale** proper and a visit to the fascinating church there. So, sticking with it, we head straight across the road and up the track beside the church. We follow the faint track round to the right as it follows the wall, but then leave it where it bends left (Wp.11 111M). Easy to miss, there is a tiny, reedy tarn on our left as we veer right here. At a fork (112M), we bear right to head down to and through a gate in the wall. With walls on either side of us, we keep close to the one on our left and follow it round as it drops to the isolated fellside cottages at **Cotehow** (Wp.12 116M).

Keeping the cottages' boundary wall on our left, we go through two gates as we head down to the road. Turning left along the asphalt (Wp.13 119M), we stride out towards the church (Wp.14 123M).

The spartan interior of St. Martin's Church

This is the older of the two churches in the parish of **Martindale** – the so-called 'new' church of **St Peter**, where we parked, was built in 1880; this one, **St Martin's**, was probably built at the end of the 16th century. On the very day that the new church was consecrated, the roof of **St Martin's** fell in during a violent storm.

The old church may not have electricity, but it has plenty of character, with its stone flagged floor, whitewashed walls and exposed beams. The font is thought to be part of a Roman altar and probably stood at a wayside shrine on 'High Street', the Roman road that crosses the tops of the fells nearby. Don't forget to have a look at the eerie, sprawling yew tree in the churchyard - it's an amazing 1,300 years old.

(Subsequent timings don't take a look around the church into consideration.) Leaving the church, we turn right along the road. Ignoring one road off to the left, we stroll up to a T-junction where we turn right (Wp.15 132M) to walk the 200 yards back to **St Peter's Church**.

The **Martindale** road being a dead end, when you drive back to civilisation after the walk, you will have to pass through or at least very close to **Pooley Bridge**, an ideal spot for a drink and a pub meal.

There can't be many routes in the Lakes that give walkers such fantastic views for so little effort. The road and track up on to the moorland above **Pooley Bridge** climb at a gentle angle to a high point of just 324 metres; and the descent is just as easy.

This is the first of our routes using the **Ullswater** 'steamer' - we walk out from **Pooley Bridge** and then catch the boat back from **Howtown**. You shouldn't experience any problems with timings if you're doing this walk in the peak summer period - boats leave **Howtown** for **Pooley Bridge** approximately every half hour between 10.55am and 5.15pm - but it's a different story in the winter when there are only two services (at 11.45am and 2.20pm). Tickets cost £4.10 for an adult, £2.05 for a child. (Based on timetables and prices for 2005. For updated information, contact Ullswater Steamers on 017684 82229 or visit the website at www.ullswater-steamers.co.uk)

Access by car: The walk starts from the Lake District National Park car park in **Pooley Bridge**, 6.5 miles south-west of **Penrith**.

Access by bus and boat: Pooley Bridge is served by the N°108, **Penrith** to **Patterdale** bus, and has a lake 'steamer' link with **Howtown** and **Glenridding** (see appendix).

Leaving the car park in **Pooley Bridge** (Wp.1 0M), we turn right to walk through the village and then bear right again at a small roundabout, towards **Howtown** and **Martindale** (Wp.2 3M). (GPS reception is intermittent between Wp.1 and Wp.4.) We go straight across the next crossroads (Wp.3 7M), towards **Hill Croft** caravan and camp site, to stroll up the quiet, tree-lined lane. As we draw level with a bench on our right, the trees kindly part to reveal a lovely view across **Ullswater** towards the high fells above **Glenridding**.

The asphalt lane ends at a gate (Wp.4 20M), which we go through to gain access to a bridleway heading towards **Helton**. Climbing very gradually, we finally leave the wide track when we reach a large cairn to the right of the path (Wp.5 37M). Turning right here, we amble across the open moorland on a constructed path.

The moorland above **Pooley Bridge**, known as **Moor Divock**, is home to a number of Bronze Age remains, including stone burial mounds and standing stones. Just before our path veers right to ford **Elder Beck**, we see one of the best examples of these remains - the stone circle known as **The Cockpit** just to the left of the path (Wp.6 43M). **The Cockpit** is about 90ft in diameter, raised on the inside of a low bank. There are 73 stones in the circle and a standing stone 300 metres to the south-west. Although thought to date back to the Bronze Age, it acquired its name in more recent history when it was used for cockfighting.

Reaching a large cairn 400 yards beyond **The Cockpit**, we cross a wide, grassy track that links up with **High Street**, the Roman road that crosses the high eastern fells. We'll save that for another day - Walk 7, in fact.

On the moorland above Pooley Bridge

This area of the Lake District, popular with horse riders, is quite different to the central fells: instead of steep, boulder-strewn slopes and craggy faces, we have gentle gradients and, in the summer, relatively luscious vegetation. The long, bubbling trill of the curlew, more at home in the **Pennines** than on Lakeland fells, can often be heard at nesting time.

The signpost above Aik Beck

Immediately after fording **Aik Beck** (Wp.7 58M), we ascend the narrower, right-hand path to a footpath sign next to a wall. Turning left towards **Howtown**, we have mixed woodland below us.

We stride out along the mostly level path with magnificent views ahead of us - the craggy, intimidating **Helvellyn** range forming a contrasting backdrop to the serene **Ullswater**. The steep slopes to our left belong to **Barton Fell**, which includes **Arthur's Pike** (532 metres).

Ullswater

Drawing level with a large building over the wall to our right as we near **Howtown**, we bear right at a fork in the path (Wp.8 99M) and drop down to a small gate. (GPS reception is intermittent from this gate until the end of the walk.) Going through, we follow the narrow path round to the left of the static caravan and through another small gate to gain access to a field, which we descend diagonally to a gate beside the road (Wp.9 103M).

To get to the pier to catch the 'steamer' back to **Pooley Bridge**, we turn left along the road and then cross over to go through a pedestrian gate at the lakeshore. This woody path soon leads to the pier (Wp.10 105M), where there is a handy shelter should you need to escape the elements while you wait.

The steamer leaving Howtown

Alternatively, if you feel like you're only just getting into your stride, you can set out on Walk 7, which starts here at the **Howtown** pier and ends back at the **Pooley Bridge** car park. This makes for a lovely, long summer's day excursion, but it does mean you'll miss out on the boat ride across **Ullswater**.

The Ullswater Navigation and Transit Company Limited started operating services on the lake in 1859, carrying mail, provisions and passengers. Two nineteenth century 'steamers' still operate - the Raven and the Lady of The Lake - although both were converted to diesel in the 1930s. A third boat, the Lady Dorothy, was brought over from Guernsey in March 2001 and restored by local boat builder Frank Howard.

Once back in **Pooley Bridge**, there are plenty of places to grab a bite to eat or just have a quick drink, including three pubs; **The Sun Inn**, **The Pooley Bridge Inn** and **The Crown Inn**, and two cafés; **Treetops** and **Granny Dowbekin's Tearooms**.

4 GOWBARROW

It often seems that some of the best views in the Lakes are from the minor tops. **Gowbarrow**, at only 481 metres, is a good example. Heading up past **Aira Force** at first, this route does a circuit of the top of the fell. It's a generally pleasant excursion as we visit the summit and then come round the eastern side of the fell, but it's when we reach the southern edge that we stop in our tracks. The view down **Ullswater** towards the **Helvellyn** range is magnificent; I don't like to use the word 'breathtaking' too often, but it's hard to resist that sharp intake of breath as the lake is fully revealed.

Access by car: The walk starts at the National Trust car park beside **Aira Force** (GR NY400200) at the junction of the A5091 and A592, 13 miles SE of **Keswick**.

Access by bus: Aira Force is served all year round by bus 108 from **Penrith** to **Patterdale** and, in the summer, by bus 208, **Keswick** to **Patterdale** (see appendix).

Going through the gap in the National Trust stone construction at the far end of the car park (Wp.1 0M), we soon hear the waters of **Aira Beck**, now having spent much of its 'force' and on its peaceful way to **Ullswater**. Surrounded by ancient yews and towering conifers, we bear left away from some iron railings to slowly ascend, with the beck on our right, to a bench (Wp.2 8M). Turning right, we plummet down the steep stone staircase to the base of the powerful falls, feeling the spray from the water even on calm days. (GPS reception is poor in the **Aira Force** gorge.)

Crossing the bridge, we immediately turn left up another steep, stone stairway, joining a path coming in from the right; here, a tiny detour will bring us to a humpback bridge on our left for a breathtaking view down the falls.

Back on the main path, there's quite a bit of clambering to be done as we wend our way upstream with the beck on our left. Another path comes in from our right (24M) and we then bear right at a fork just above a small wooden bridge (Wp.3).

The woods start to thin out after we pass through one gate and then disappear entirely after a second one.

Reaching a blue footpath sign just before another gate, we turn right (Wp.4 36M) to start climbing on a faint path. Having crossed a ladder stile, we battle our way uphill, sometimes having to clamber over rocky outcrops, sometimes taking two steps forward and one step back as we slither around on the muddy ground.

Gowbarrow trig point

We keep the wall on our immediate left until, after 25 minutes of uphill slog, the path finally levels off slightly and we can see the trig point just off to our right. Swinging round to the right on an obvious but sometimes boggy path, we make a beeline for the summit. There are plenty of nooks and crannies at the top (Wp.5 66M) where we can rest out of the wind and enjoy the views, which include **Helvellyn** (SW), **Blencathra** (NW) and our first glimpse of **Ullswater**.

Picking up a path running in a NE direction, we quickly drop down from the summit knoll, one of the many small, heathery knobbles that make up the top of **Gowbarrow**. Bounding along, we weave in and out of the knolls as the path starts to swing round to the south-east.

Lakeland primroses

With the sparkling waters of **Ullswater** ahead of us, we bear right at a ruined building (Wp.6 82M) to follow a narrow path around the eastern side of the fell. An easy, two-minute climb brings us to a delightful dell, which, in springtime, is carpeted with wildflowers, including primroses.

No daffodils, I'm afraid, although the woodland on the lower slopes of **Gowbarrow** is said to have inspired William Wordsworth to write his most famous lines. Having walked through the woods with him on April 15, 1802, his sister Dorothy noted in her diary, "I never saw daffodils so beautiful. They grew among the mossy stones about and about them, some rested their heads upon these stones as on a pillow for weariness and the rest tossed and reeled and danced and seemed as if they verily laughed with the wind that blew upon them over the lake, they looked so gay ever dancing ever changing." Two years later, William used Dorothy's observations as the basis of *that* poem.

Fifteen minutes beyond the dell - although who's clock-watching on such a wonderful path? - we bear left at a fork (Wp.7) and then, in another five minutes, we're stopped in our tracks.

Coming round the side of a crag, we're suddenly faced with one of the most magnificent panoramas in the eastern Lakes.

Ullswater

The western expanse of **Ullswater** is revealed, blue and inviting, with the dark, craggy **Helvellyn** range in the background, providing a perfect counterpoint to the water's serenity. Another 45 yards and we come to a perfectly placed bench, a chance to sit and admire.

Always with that sumptuous view ahead, we continue on a level path for a further ten minutes and then descend gently to a gate (Wp.8 128M). Going through, we turn left to descend through woodland to a bridge over **Aira Beck**.

Having crossed, we climb the steps on the other side to bear left through a gap in some iron railings. It's now a five-minute woodland stroll back to the car park and then off to **Aira Force**'s teashop which serves a mean cappucino.

Aira Beck

Pikeawassa? Who's ever heard of it? The highest point on a ridge known as **Steel Knotts**, it is one of those lesser-known little tops close to the edge of the Lake District and, thanks to its obscurity, there's a good chance we'll have it all to ourselves.

It makes for a decent half-day walk. There's an energetic but short pull to get to the 432 metre summit, and then a lonely ridge walk that opens out to empty moorland. Our return is via the delightful valley of **Fusedale**.

Access by car: you'll need to drive to the start of the walk, which is **St Peter's Church** in **Martindale** (GR NY 435191), 4.4 miles SW of **Pooley Bridge**.

St Peter's Church

Starting from the church (Wp.1 0M), we walk up the wide lane to the right of the building. As soon as the church wall ends, we head up the steep, grassy bank immediately in front of us (Wp.2 1M) – ignoring the clear, wide track that heads off to the right.

The path swings to the left and we obediently follow it as it ascends slightly and then drops down to a clearer track coming in from the right (Wp.3 6M). Bearing left, we saunter along this lovely bridleway for almost half a mile (700 yards) with the slopes of **Pikeawassa** to our right and sparkling views of **Ullswater** ahead.

Ullswater, seen from Pikeawassa

Finding the path on to **Pikeawassa** can be tricky, so we need to keep our wits about us now. We pass a concrete bench and then a wooden bench. Beyond the wooden bench we need to start counting manhole covers to find our route on to the fell. We pass one large and then one small manhole cover to the left of the path and then a further two large manhole covers. At the second of these, as we reach a tree on the other side of the drystone wall to our left, we turn right to head straight up the north-eastern ridge of **Pikeawassa** (Wp.4 19M). The path is just to the right of a small rocky outcrop, but it can be hard to make out, especially in summer when it is hidden by the bracken.

The path is faint - a good sign, as it means we're likely to have the next few miles pretty much to ourselves. We slog our way upwards. It's a steep path, some of it making use of grassy rakes between the crags, but it's never quite a scramble.

After almost 25 minutes of climbing, the path levels slightly, providing welcome relief for our screaming calf muscles. Walking along the western side of the ridge, we are able to see popular little **Hallin Fell** (see Walk 2) to our right; the nobbly brown top of **Gowbarrow** (Walk 4) beyond that; and, behind them in the distance, mighty **Blencathra** (Walk 21).

We climb gently on grass up to the cairn marking the first summit (Wp.5 54M) and then stride out along the gorgeous ridge path towards the tor-like rocky outcrop marking the true summit (Wp.6 62M).

The rocks at the summit

You can clamber up on to the rocks easily, but trying to stand on the razor-sharp top of the highest pinnacle is tricky in anything but the daintiest of shoes.

Beyond the top, we drop down a grassy slope to a wall, which we cross via a stone stile (Wp.7 70M), and then bear left with the wall on our left

We ignore one path off to the left and veer away from the wall to meet a more obvious path coming in from the right (Wp.8 73M).

Bearing left, we climb gently and are soon able to see a red-roofed bungalow down in the valley to our right. This is known as 'The Bungalow' and was the hunting lodge of the popular but eccentric 'Yellow' Earl of Lonsdale (Hugh Lowther). He entertained the Kaiser here in 1895 and 1902. On one occasion, knowing that the Kaiser liked to shoot rabbits, he instructed his keepers to net as many as possible and conceal them in some nearby woodland. On approaching the trees with the Kaiser, he told his fellow huntsman that rabbits were often seen in the area. He then gave the word for the dogs to be sent into the woods and the keepers released the rabbits. Within seconds, hundreds of rabbits came running from the woods, providing the Kaiser with plenty of target practice.

The steep slopes heading down to our right soon give way to open country, more reminiscent of the **Pennines** than the Lake District - but then, that's hardly surprising, we are on the eastern fells here; England's 'backbone' is just a short jump away across the **Eden Valley**.

Curving slowly to the left across sometimes soggy ground, we go through a gap in a drystone wall and then ford **Fusedale Beck** (Wp.9 97M). Once around the back of the ruined building just above the beck, we turn left to begin the descent of lonely **Fusedale**. Having crossed a tributary beck as it plummets noisily down the steep-sided gully of **Groove Gill** (Wp.10 107M), our way down gets steeper for a short while and then eases off again as we reach another ruined building with a handy bench in front of it (Wp.11 113M).

The delights of **Fusedale** continue as we slowly approach a solitary farmhouse. We gingerly cross a narrow plank bridge (Wp.12 124M), then a minute later, as we draw level with an impressive rocky gully in the fellside to our right, we bear left (Wp.13) away from the wide track and head down towards the footbridge on our left. We cross (Wp.14 127M) and then bear right to follow the gently gurgling beck.

Sign at the re-crossing of the beck

Re-crossing the beck a few minutes later , we turn left on to a concrete track (Wp.15) and stay with it until, just before a cattle grid, we reach a signpost to the right of the track (Wp16 139M). Turning left towards **Martindale Hause**, we amble along a grassy bridleway that we soon recognise as the one we followed around the base of **Pikeawassa** at the beginning of the walk.

Having passed the now familiar concrete slab and manhole cover marking the beginning of the day's climb (Wp.4), we retrace our steps back to the church, remembering to turn right at Wp.3 (155M).

6 BOREDALE ROUND: PLACE FELL & BEDA FELL

You won't find many horseshoe walks as quiet as the **Boredale** Round; in fact, you won't find many people who've even heard of this route. Although it takes in the increasingly popular **Place Fell** (657 metres), after leaving **Boredale Hause** to head up on to **Beda Fell** (509 metres), you're unlikely to see many other walkers.

The climb on to **Place Fell** is well spaced out, making it relatively easy, and the views from the top across to **Helvellyn** are magnificent. In winter, in particular, the snow and ice clinging precariously to the eastern cliffs of England's third highest mountain are an amazing sight.

There's a steep descent down to **Boredale Hause**, followed by a gentle climb up on to the quiet, undulating ridge of **Beda Fell** - keep an eye out for red deer up here. One Christmas Day a few years ago, I surprised two beautiful deer - one of them a stag - on **Beda Fell**. With the wind blowing straight at me, they hadn't been aware of my approach until I'd got within just a few feet of them.

On a relatively short and low-level walk such as this one, you're unlikely to need an escape route. However, in the case of an emergency, you can cut the walk short at **Boredale Hause**. Simply turn left along the first clear path that you come to when you reach the pass. A steep track down leads to the valley road and back to **Garth Heads**, a distance of 2¼ miles. Turning right at **Boredale Hause** will give an even faster descent - into **Patterdale**, just 0.9 miles away.

3/4   3½ H   6.3 miles/10.1km   680m / 680m   0

Garth Heads

Access by car: The walk starts at **Garth Heads** in **Boredale** (GR NY427185), 5.2 miles south-west of **Pooley Bridge**. There is some roadside parking on the single-track **Boredale** road, but please park considerately by not blocking gates, passing places or junctions. The nearest car park is at **St Peter's Church** in **Martindale**, a 0.8-mile walk from **Garth Heads**.

Facing up the valley, we turn right at the public footpath sign beside the buildings at **Garth Heads** (Wp.1 0M). Crossing a stile beside a gate, we stroll down the clear track to **Boredale Beck**. The track ends at a ford, but wet feet can be avoided by crossing via the slab-stone bridge just to our left (Wp.2 ¼M). Once over the beck, we squelch our way across soggy ground (getting our boots wet after all!) to the gate in the top, right-hand corner of the enclosure. Picking up a track on the other side of the gate, we head up towards a stone barn where waymarkers indicate that we keep the building on our right as we plod up the gentle incline to cross the double stile at the top (8M).

So far, so easy. But looking straight up now, we can see a faint, grassy line rising very steeply through the bracken.

This is our route ahead. But fear not; it's a short climb, just 11 metres of vertical gain in 50 yards.

At the top of this initial climb we meet a clearer path (Wp.3 10M), along which we turn left, climbing at a much easier angle. As we plod slowly uphill, we look down the isolated valley of **Boredale**, home only to a few farms, some house martins and the occasional swallow.

The gentle climb onto Place Fell

After nearly 15 minutes of gentle ascent, we swing right as the grassy path becomes more stony and the gradient steepens. Reaching another track coming in from our right (Wp.4 30M), we bear left to continue our climb, soon finding ourselves on the open fell as we drop down to a stone enclosure in a small depression (Wp.5 46M).

Still heading in a mostly SW direction, we walk uphill on an increasingly craggy path with ever-improving views both behind and in front of us. Eventually, after the steepest pull of the day, we reach the trig point on **Place Fell** (Wp.6 83M). It's a popular little top - if you're here on a summer Sunday, you'll probably be sharing the summit with lots of families who have slogged up the steep path from **Patterdale** and are now admiring the fantastic views.

To the east you can see the **Pennines** and the **Pooley Bridge** end of **Ullswater**; then there's **Blencathra** (NW), the craggy **Helvellyn** range (WSW), **St Sunday Crag** to the south of that (see picture on the next page) and **High**

Street (SE). Moving away from the trig point towards the western edge of the summit, we can also look down to **Glenridding**.

Helvellyn & St. Sunday Crag from the summit

Coming away from the summit crag (S), we pick up a clear, level path along the western edge of the fell. To avoid a loose, unpleasant scramble down a badly eroded section of path, 360 yards after the trig point we turn right along a faint path (Wp.7).

Striding out with wonderful views down to **Glenridding** and **Ullswater** to our right, you may be lucky enough to spot deer grazing on the steep slopes below; sadly though, you won't see any wild goats; Wordsworth tells us that the country's last flock disappeared from **Place Fell** in 1805.

Heading down to Boredale Hause

We soon meet up with the main path again (Wp.8 91M) and turn right. Despite missing out the worst of it, this is still a badly eroded route and there's a long way to go to the easier ground at the pass. Slip-sliding our way down the steep, loose path, the knees cry out in triumph and gratitude as we finally reach **Boredale Hause** (114M). Crossing one clear path, we reach a small, drystone construction and turn left along a very faint path heading away from its far corner (Wp.9 115M).

Soon crossing another clear path, we keep straight ahead. Ambling easily along this gently rising path, we leave the busy routes of **Place Fell** and **Boredale Hause** far behind as we make our way up on to the lonely ridge of **Beda Fell**. We reach the open felltop at a junction of paths marked by a small cairn (Wp.10 138M). Turning left, we stride out along the peaceful ridge. The small fell to our right as we set off is **The Nab** (576 metres), an important part of the ancient **Martindale Deer Forest**. Managed by **Dalemain** Estates as a sporting reserve, it is the only red deer forest of its kind left in England. Late in the year, you may hear an eerie noise coming from that direction – the call of the stags as rutting season begins.

Further along the ridge, we catch a glimpse of some red-roofed buildings in the valley to our right. One of these, 'The Bungalow', was the hunting lodge of the Earl of Lonsdale, the boxing fan after whom the famous title belt is named. (For more information on The Bungalow, see Walk 5, **Pikeawassa**.)

Rollercoaster-like, the ridge path undulates constantly as we make our way to the top of **Beda Head** (Wp.11 170M), marked by a small cairn (see photo in the next page).

Dropping down from here, a large cairn can be seen on a hummock just ahead. Avoiding the climb up to this, we skirt around the hummock, keeping it on our left, then drop down to a junction of faint paths (Wp.12 178M).

Beda Head

On Beda Fell

Turning right (NE), our way ahead is now mostly downhill, although we still have one little knobble to get over.

We finally leave the ridge at a crossing of paths at a welcome metal bench (Wp.13 206M). Turning left, we shoot down the steep, grassy path and reach the road at **Garth Heads** where the walk began (Wp.1 210M).

... a welcome metal bench ...

7 LOADPOT HILL

This is the second of our routes using the **Ullswater** 'steamer'. Having parked at the Lake District National Park car park in **Pooley Bridge**, we get the delightful ferry from just outside the village to **Howtown**, walk up quiet **Fusedale** and then on to the Roman road known as **High Street**. This moorland, dotted with historic remains and reaching a height of 671 metres at **Loadpot Hill**, is more like the nearby **Pennines** than the Lake District. And, as if to prove the point, England's backbone is constantly in view as we descend gently to **Pooley Bridge**.

Access to Howtown by boat only: The walk starts from **Ullswater** 'steamer' pier in **Howtown** (see appendix for details). Alternatively, you can walk from **Pooley Bridge** using the description for Walk 3 to create a 13½-mile circuit.

Access to Pooley Bridge: For information on how to get to **Pooley Bridge** by car or bus, see Walk 3.

Having disembarked from the boat and walked down the pier (Wp.1 0M), we cross the small footbridge to our right, heading towards **Sandwick**. (GPS reception is poor in the woody area near the lake.) We are treated to a short section of delightful lakeshore walking before we go through two gates to come to a surfaced lane (Wp.2 2M). Turning left here, we soon come to a road, which we go straight across (Wp.3 4M).

We now enter the isolated hamlet of **Howtown** and, as we pass a large white building on our left, we follow the lane as it swings right to head gently uphill. (GPS reception is intermittent from here until Wp.4.) The babbling stream to our left is **Fusedale Beck**, which will keep us company for the next 1.4 miles.

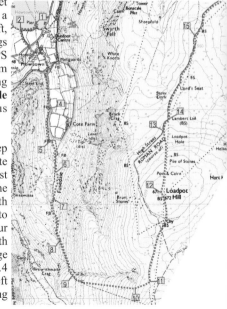

Crossing a cattle grid, we keep straight ahead on the concrete track towards **Wether Hill**. Just before the next cattle grid at the entrance to **Cote Farm**, and with the steep slopes leading up to **Pikeawassa** (see Walk 5) on our right, we turn right at a footpath sign to cross a small stone bridge over **Fusedale Beck** (Wp.4 21M). Once across, we bear left along the narrow path heading upstream.

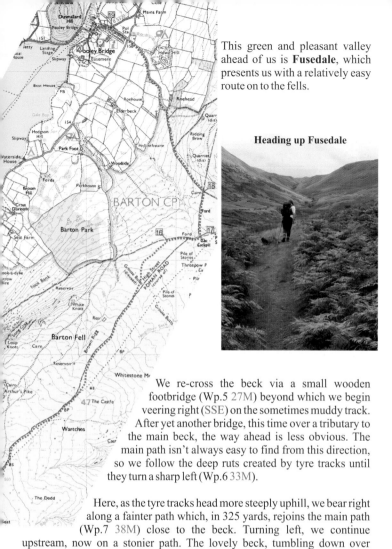

This green and pleasant valley ahead of us is **Fusedale**, which presents us with a relatively easy route on to the fells.

Heading up Fusedale

We re-cross the beck via a small wooden footbridge (Wp.5 27M) beyond which we begin veering right (SSE) on the sometimes muddy track. After yet another bridge, this time over a tributary to the main beck, the way ahead is less obvious. The main path isn't always easy to find from this direction, so we follow the deep ruts created by tyre tracks until they turn a sharp left (Wp.6 33M).

Here, as the tyre tracks head more steeply uphill, we bear right along a fainter path which, in 325 yards, rejoins the main path (Wp.7 38M) close to the beck. Turning left, we continue upstream, now on a stonier path. The lovely beck, tumbling down over smooth, water-worn boulders, enlivens what could otherwise be a monotonous climb.

Beyond a ruined building with a handy bench outside it (Wp.8 47M), our route ahead gets a little steeper. Exactly 100 yards after crossing **Groove Gill**, a subsidiary gully to the main dale, we leave the clear path by turning left along a faint path heading steeply uphill through the grass between two small rocky outcrops (Wp.9 63M). Although it seems little more than a sheep trod, this faint line, which runs almost parallel with **Groove Gill**, will eventually lead us on to the Roman road, **High Street**.

It's a slow, steep plod upwards, demanding enough for us to justify some time out to turn round and enjoy the suddenly much-improved view of the high fells - **Blencathra**, **Skiddaw**, **Helvellyn**, **St Sunday Crag** and **Fairfield** to name but a few.

Fell ponies

You may be lucky enough to catch a glimpse of the ponies that roam these gently-sloping eastern fells. As we draw level with the head of the gully on our left, our path suddenly swings left and the gradient eases (Wp.10 89M). Another five minutes and we reach the broad ridge path (Wp.11), along which we turn left. This is **High Street**, the audacious, high-level Roman road that linked the forts of Galava (**Ambleside**) and Brovacum (**Brougham**).

Turning our backs on the craggy Lake District fells, we stride out along this wonderful path with the **Pennines** filling the horizon to our right. Reaching the trig point at the top of **Loadpot Hill** (Wp.12 102M), we are treated to far-reaching views in all directions. This is a great place to linger and soak up the views.

Trig point on Loadpot Hill

We leave the summit via the clear, wide track heading north. This really is the best of both worlds - you feel like you're walking on the lonely **Pennine** moors, with their wide open spaces, big views and a wonderful sense of solitude, but just to the west are some of England's most spectacularly craggy mountains. As we lose height, we can see our path stretching on into the distance invitingly.

Boundary stone on High Street

The Roman road proper doesn't actually go to the summit of **Loadpot Hill** but, as we drop down the northern side of the fell, we come to a junction with the ancient route (Wp.13 110M), along which we turn right.

Almost 180 yards after this junction, we pass an upright stone just to the right of the path (Wp.14 112M). Marked on OS maps as **Lambert Lad**, it's thought to predate the boundary stones that we see elsewhere along **High Street**; it may even be an original Roman marker.

These fells, apparently featureless at first glance, are alive with history. Just beyond **Lambert Lad**, we cross the source of **Swarth Beck** and just below us is a tiny stone circle. With many stones missing and none left standing, it's barely recognisable as a stone circle and takes a bit of finding. With a more interesting Bronze Age site to come later in the walk, it hardly seems worth the effort of a detour - unless, of course, you're a stone circle enthusiast.

Bearing right at a fork in the track (Wp.15 131M), we can see the town of **Penrith** straight ahead and, to the right, is **Cross Fell**, the highest point on the **Pennines**. Almost 700 yards beyond the fork, we ignore the tyre tracks heading off to the right and keep to the main track. As we lose height, we encounter one or two boggy patches where you need to keep your wits about you to ensure that you don't lose the path.

Clouds over The Cockpit

Reaching a junction of paths at a cairn, we turn right (Wp.16 163M). We soon ford shallow **Elder Beck** and then, as the track swings left, we pass a stone circle to our right (Wp.17 167M). This is **The Cockpit** (for full details, see Walk 3). Turning left at the next path junction, marked by a large cairn (Wp.18 173M), we head downhill on a broad, stony bridleway with views ahead of **Ullswater**.

Once we've gone through a gate near the beginning of the driveway to the buildings at **Roehead**, we continue downhill on a surfaced lane. (GPS reception is intermittent along this lane and in **Pooley Bridge**.) We go straight across at a crossroads and then turn left at a mini roundabout on the edge of the village (Wp.19 207M). The car park (Wp.20) is just on the other side of the village now, a three-minute stroll away. Along the way, we pass three pubs; **The Sun Inn**, **The Pooley Bridge Inn** and **The Crown Inn**, and two cafés; **Treetops** and **Granny Dowbekin's Tearooms**.

8 HIGH STREET FROM HARTSOP

High Street (828 metres) is the highest of the eastern fells and yet it was across this long, grass-topped mountain that the Romans marched their legions on their way between the forts of Galava (**Ambleside**) and Brovacum (**Brougham**). The highest Roman road in the country, the 25-mile route is still used as a footpath.

Although we'll be following in the footsteps of those ancient soldiers for part of our way, there's no need for a route march on *our* walk – unless you feel the urge. We start at **Hartsop**, 2.1 miles south of **Patterdale** on the A592, and follow the long, glacial valley of **Pasture Beck** before climbing up the western flank of **Thornthwaite Crag**. It's a stiff ascent, sometimes on loose ground, but we're rewarded with wonderful views and a gentle stroll across to **High Street** and, beyond that, **Angle Tarn**.

4/5   5H   10 miles/16.1km   827m   827m   0

Access by car: Most of the year, you have no choice but to drive to the start of the walk, which is the car park at the far, eastern end of the hamlet of **Hartsop** (GR NY410131). Driving south along the A592, the turning for Hartsop is 3 miles outside Glenridding on your left.

Access by bus: On summer weekends, the Kirkstone Rambler bus passes **Hartsop** on its route between **Bowness-on-Windermere** and **Glenridding** (see appendix).

Going through the kissing gate at the top end of the car park (Wp.1 0M), we turn right immediately, towards **Pasture Beck**, and go through a large gate. Crossing the stream, we bear left at the fork immediately after the bridge (1M) and keep to the clear track as it swings left beyond the next gate/stile (2M).

At the start, Hartsop Dodd ahead

Looking to our left (8M), we can see the remains of the stone piers that formed part of the 30-foot water wheel used to drain **Low Hartsop** lead mine, abandoned in 1878. Another five minutes into the walk and we lose the drystone wall that's been on our left almost since crossing the bridge (Wp.2 13M).

Replacing it as our companion is **Pasture Beck**, gently tumbling its way down the valley to join other streams on their way to nearby **Ullswater**. Our route ahead is obvious now – a long, pretty valley carved out between **Hartsop Dodd** (618 metres) to our right and **Gray Crag** (710 metres) to our left.

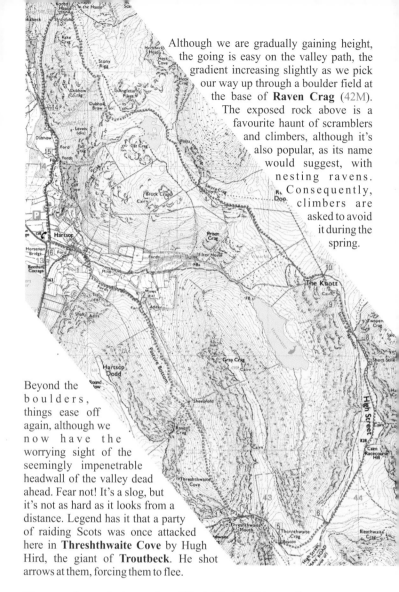

Although we are gradually gaining height, the going is easy on the valley path, the gradient increasing slightly as we pick our way up through a boulder field at the base of **Raven Crag** (42M). The exposed rock above is a favourite haunt of scramblers and climbers, although it's also popular, as its name would suggest, with nesting ravens. Consequently, climbers are asked to avoid it during the spring.

Beyond the boulders, things ease off again, although we now have the worrying sight of the seemingly impenetrable headwall of the valley dead ahead. Fear not! It's a slog, but it's not as hard as it looks from a distance. Legend has it that a party of raiding Scots was once attacked here in **Threshthwaite Cove** by Hugh Hird, the giant of **Troutbeck**. He shot arrows at them, forcing them to flee.

There are plenty of other stories of Hugh Hird and his amazing strength and appetite, including a royal encounter. When sent by Lord Dacre with a message for the king, he astonished the royal household by eating a whole sheep for his dinner.

Trudging up the constructed path at the valley end, we bear left at a fork as we approach the top (Wp.3 76M). The neat stairway soon ends, but there are cairns to guide us and, before you know it, we're at **Threshthwaite Mouth**, the saddle between **Threshthwaite Crag** and **Thornthwaite Crag** looking down into **Troutbeck**. And what a view! No wonder Hugh Hird felt the need to defend his beautiful valley! The lake in the distance is **Windermere** and beyond that is **Morecambe Bay**.

Crossing the wall, we reach a clear path (Wp.4 80M) where we turn left to begin the steep pull up to **Thornthwaite Crag**. There is a short, easy section of scrambling early in the climb, but this can be easily avoided by using a narrow path off to the left and then coming back round to the main path just above the rocky outcrop. Scrabbling our weary way up the loose path, it is best to chart a zigzagging course up the steepest sections.

At last, having climbed for almost half an hour from the saddle, we see the beacon that marks the top of **Thornthwaite Crag** (784 metres). The views from here are truly amazing, particularly to the west where the **Scafell** range stands out craggy against the horizon; further north, and closer in, are the complicated twists and turns on the eastern cliffs of **Fairfield** and the **Helvellyn** range.

Going through the gap in the wall behind the beacon (Wp.5 112M), we stride out on the wide, stony track that heads off in an ESE direction, soon swinging round to the NE. The body of water down in the valley to our left is **Hayeswater**, which we will see from a different angle later in the walk. Reaching a dilapidated wall (Wp.6 121M), we leave the track by turning right. Following the wall, we keep it on our left when it turns a sharp left after 35 yards.

On High Street

Ambling along this sometimes peaty, but mostly grassy path, we are barely aware that we are still gaining height until we suddenly stumble upon the trig point at the top of **High Street** (Wp.7 135M). This flat summit area is also known as **Racecourse Hill** because shepherds and farmers used to hold their annual meets (including horse races) here. They eventually moved down to **Mardale** - until the valley was flooded to make way for **Haweswater** reservoir.

To our right, we now have a clear view of the **Pennines**. To snatch a glimpse of **Blea Water** down the surprisingly craggy, eastern face of **High Street**, we can take a detour to the edge of the fell. You may, if extremely lucky, also catch a rare sight of this area's most famous resident – England's last remaining golden eagle. After an absence of about 150 years, a pair of eagles returned to the Lake District in 1969. Sadly, the female bird, the second to occupy the **Haweswater** site, died in 2004. The male, however, is still in the area and is putting on spectacular display flights, probably in the hope of attracting a new mate.

Back on the main path, we continue following the wall on our left in a southerly direction. Strolling down this lovely grassy path, we eventually rejoin the track that we left at Wp.6 when it crosses the wall (Wp.8 150M). With the wall still on our left, we keep straight ahead, ignoring a path off to the right in 100 yards. A quarter of a mile beyond this ignored turn, we leave the main path (Wp.9 157M) to stay with our silent companion, the wall, as it swings a sharp left up the side of **The Knott**.

It's a short pull to the top (739 metres), marked by an enormous cairn, quite out of proportion to the significance of this little bump. Staying with the companionable wall as it swings right, we shoot downhill, turning left at a clear track (Wp.10 167M). We say goodbye to our faithful friend as we cross the wall to head down the stony track. Ignoring any paths off to the left, we drop down to a boggy area, the soggiest sections of which we cross via the carefully placed stones. Climbing out of the depression, if you look behind, you'll again see **Hayeswater**, as promised earlier.

The undulating path that we're on is part of Wainwright's Coast to Coast walk. This wonderful, 190-mile excursion starts at **St Bees** on Cumbria's Irish Sea coast and crosses three national parks - the Lake District, the Yorkshire Dales and the North York Moors - on its way to **Robin Hood's Bay** on the North Sea coast. Wainwright devised the long-distance route in 1973, having been inspired by the opening of the Pennine Way in 1965.

We catch our first glimpse of **Angle Tarn** just after passing through a small gate (Wp.11 211M). Resisting the urge to leap into its inky black waters, we drop down to the east side of the tarn and then curve round to the left (W) as we climb away from it. Ignoring a faint path off up to the right, we stay on the level and swing round to the right (NE) to traverse the fellside.

Angle Tarn

Looking towards Brothers Water

This is a lovely section of path - narrow with steep drops to the left, but not exposed enough to cause problems for anyone but the most faint-hearted. But, alas, it is over all too soon - after just six minutes, we start dropping down towards **Boredale Hause**.

Reaching a flat, grassy area at a junction of paths just above a decrepit sheepfold to our left (Wp.12 254M), we turn left and then immediately left again (Wp.13) to head more steeply downhill. The path is very loose in places, so you'll need to watch your footing.

There's a definite sense of returning to civilisation as we see **Patterdale** and various scattered hamlets below us and the sound of barking farm dogs drifts up to us on the breeze. Dropping down to a T-junction (Wp.14 279M), we turn left along the wide, level track. Ambling pleasantly along, we cross a bridge just below a small waterfall and go through a gate (Wp.15 286M) to gain access to a rough lane that soon goes over to asphalt. At a road junction with a white building on our right (Wp.16 295M), we turn left to stroll the 500 yards through the pretty stone-built hamlet of **Hartsop** back to the car park (Wp.1 300M

This gentle stroll across low, bracken-covered moorland makes a pleasant summer's evening stroll – possibly before a visit to the nearby stone circle at **Castlerigg**. Alternatively, it can be used as a gentle extension to the **High Rigg** walk (Walk 10). Together, they form a figure of eight.

St. John's Church

Access by car: There's a small parking area opposite the isolated **St John's Church** (GR NY306225) 3½ miles south-east of **Keswick,** just off the B5322. The current church of **St John's-in-the-Vale** dates from 1845, although there's been a chapel on the site since the 16th century.

Dragging ourselves away from the parking area (Wp.1 0M) with its captivating view of **Blencathra**, we stroll down the road with the church on our right. Going through a large gate (6M), we

Looking towards Blencathra

continue along the road until it bends sharply to the right (Wp.2 9M). Leaving it here, we turn left along a lane towards **Row End** – and there's that view of **Blencathra** again. Spellbinding, isn't it?

Passing in front of the white farmhouse, we go through the left-hand of the two gates ahead of us (Wp.3 14M). Using the green gap between the tufts of long grass - and dodging the sheep as we go - we stroll across the field towards a group of trees slightly to our left. Once past them, we cross a small stream to head for the steps up to the drystone wall to our left.

Climbing the steps and going through the gate at the top of them (Wp.4 19M), we turn right to amble along the grassy path with a wall on our right. On reaching the buildings at **Shundraw**, which include an interesting early eighteenth century farmhouse, we go through the large gate to gain access to a grassy lane. This soft carpet of green leads us around the back of the buildings to another gate, through which we walk to get to the road (Wp.5 23M).

Turning left, we stride up the quiet road until, 320 yards beyond **Shundraw**, we come to a gate (Wp.6 28M) with several walkers' signs attached to it that suggest a path lies on the other side. Sadly, when I last did this walk, there wasn't actually a signpost – maybe that omission has since been put right. Despite the lack of signposting, we go through the gate and head up the faint, grassy track that ascends diagonally across the field before veering back round to the right.

Tewet Tarn

At the top of the field, we go through a gap in the wall to gain a clearer track, but this too soon dwindles to very little as we approach pretty **Tewet Tarn**. Our way ahead is unclear now, but if you look to the left of the tarn, you'll see a gate surrounded by barbed wire. To the left of that is a stile in the wall that will give us access to more open country. Crossing it (Wp.7 36M), we pick up a faint, grassy track that heads briefly towards the water's edge.

A heron at the edge of the tarn

On a sunny summer's day, this is a great spot to stop for a picnic. There are ducks on the water and lapwings wheeling and diving in the skies above, sounding for all the world like those Space Invader machines from the 1980s. *Tewet* is, in fact, another name for the lapwing. If you're lucky (and quiet), you may also see a heron fishing in the reedy shallows on the other side of the tiny tarn.

Beyond the tarn (if you can tear yourself away from this peaceful place), we veer SSW along the faint track to cross a stile in a fence. Having squelched our way across a small damp patch, we climb the easy, grassy slope to reach the highest point on the walk (250 metres).

Our route ahead is obvious, although it can be a little damp in places after wet weather. Crossing a drystone wall, we head for the buildings at the base of **High Rigg**. As we approach the wall near the church and our parking area, we turn left (Wp.8 57M) off the main path and down towards a signpost beside a stile in the wall. Crossing, we turn left to find ourselves just feet away from where we started.

Now, having finished the walk - and such a short one at that - can you resist the temptation to continue on up **High Rigg** as described in Walk 10?

10 HIGH RIGG

Although the summit of **High Rigg** is only 357 metres above sea level, its short, undulating ridge provides a wonderful walk amid beautiful mountain scenery –a sort of Lake District in miniature. In fact, this is a great route for introducing young people to fell-walking. The hard work is over early in the walk with a brief, but steep climb up to the summit cairn. The ridge path is easy to follow, although it does become a little boggy in one place, and the return route follows the pretty valley of **St John's Beck** through woodland and beside pastureland.

Although the walk itself takes only about two and a half hours, allow a little extra time for a visit to the friendly, inexpensive walkers' tea-room at **Low Bridge End Farm**, about two-thirds of the way into the route.

2/3   2½ H   5 miles/8km   375m / 375m   3

St. John's Church graveyard

Access by car:
There's a small parking area opposite the isolated **St John's Church** (GR NY 306225) 3.5 miles south-east of **Keswick,** just off the B5322. The current church of **St John's-in-the-Vale** dates from 1845, although there has been a chapel on the site since the 16th century. The churchyard contains the grave of the nineteenth century Cumberland dialect poet John Richardson.

With the church (Wp.1 0M) on our left, we walk along the road and, as soon as we pass the recently refurbished diocesan youth centre, we turn left. Heading straight up the narrow, muddy path we can take either branch when it forks around the back of the building and at the top of the initial climb, we head for the small gate in the wall (4M).

Once through, we plod up the northern ridge of **High Rigg** - a short, but sharp climb. It's easy to pace ourselves as the ascent is divided into short sections, each ending at a level terrace where we can pause for a while to catch our breath. After all, we've barely had a chance to warm up before we're being called on to head uphill!

Blencathra, seen from High Rigg

The top of the ridge, marked by a cairn on top of the crag to the right of the main path, is only 28 minutes from the church.

Looking south from High Rigg summit

After visiting the summit (Wp.2) for some great views across to **Blencathra**, we head back down the crag in a southerly direction and then bear right along a grassy path that descends and winds its way across the knobbly top to the corner of a drystone wall. Ahead of us are **Thirlmere** and, up to its left, the **Helvellyn** range.

Having reached the wall, we amble gently uphill with it on our left and then aim to the right of some soggy ground in a depression straight ahead. We cross it at its driest part and bear left again around the base of a crag to regain the wall. Dropping down to a ladder stile (Wp.3 39M), we cross and saunter easily uphill away from the wall, ignoring the faint path off to the left just 50 yards beyond the stile.

Strolling along a lovely, grassy path, the blue waters of **Thirlmere** and the thick forests surrounding it urge us on. **Thirlmere** is a natural lake but was enlarged in 1894 to form a reservoir. Victorian engineers devised a system, still in use today, which allows water to flow by gravity, without any pumps, all the way from the reservoir to **Manchester**, nearly 100 miles away.

Sticking with the path as it swings round to the left, we cross a stile (Wp.4 50M) to find ourselves on a more open ridge route. Striding out with the steep scree slopes of the **Dodds** to our left and the wonderful views straight ahead, it is hard to believe we're only 300 metres above sea level. The ridge, known here as **Long Band**, ends suddenly as we veer left to drop down a steep, loose path to a gap in a wall (Wp.5 65M).

Beyond the gap, with the promise of further wonderful ridge walking ahead, we shoot up the next short incline only to have our hopes quickly dashed as the path drops away again down the fell's southern ridge.

As we career down through the Scots pines, we catch glimpses of a large, bare rockface across the valley to our left. This is **Castle Rock**, so-named because 18th century travellers on their way from **Ambleside** to **Keswick** used to see it and believe it was a castle. On approaching it, however, it turned into a simple crag. This was explained locally as being the work of the castle's guardian genie who wanted to keep strangers away. Sir Walter Scott made the vale of St John the main setting for his 'Bride of Triermain'. It's at **Castle Rock** that Sir Walter has King Arthur dallying with the fortress's fairy inhabitants while on his way to **Carlisle**.

Dropping down to a T-junction of paths (Wp.6 91M), we turn left to head along a narrow path around the side of the fell. There is a steep drop to our right down to **St John's Beck** at first, but we soon reach the valley bottom.

Twelve minutes into the valley walk, we reach **Low Bridge End Farm** (Wp.7), a friendly spot which welcomes walkers for drinks and cakes. On a warm afternoon, it's hard to resist the lure of those outside tables; in the winter, the promise of a hot drink in the conservatory wills us down the farm path.

The return along the valley

Continuing along the valley path, we stroll through pleasant woodland (where GPS reception is poor) before the way ahead opens out, allowing **Blencathra** to fill the vista ahead.

Cruelly, we have to climb away from the valley bottom in the final stages of the walk. So, with those lovely farm scones weighing us down, we trudge gradually uphill for the last mile. On reaching the road (Wp.8 148M), we turn left and plod the 110 yards back to the church (Wp.1).

Sheffield Pike is often forsaken by walkers in favour of its larger, more famous neighbours in the **Helvellyn** range. However, it is well worth a visit. This is a relatively straightforward 'up and down' walk - up the secluded valley of **Glencoyne** and on to the summit of **Sheffield Pike** (675m); then down to **Glenridding Beck** and a lakeside stroll back to the car park. The paths are easy to follow, although they can get boggy on the ridge path up to the summit cairn.

A short detour towards the end takes us into **Glenridding** for well-earned refreshments in one of the good cafés or pubs.

*in nearby **Glenridding**

Access by car: the walk starts from the National Trust car park at **Glencoyne** (GR NY386188) on the A592, 1.2 miles north of **Glenridding**.

Access by bus: Glencoyne is served all year round by bus 108 from **Penrith** and **Patterdale** and, in the summer, by bus 208, **Keswick** to **Patterdale** (see appendix).

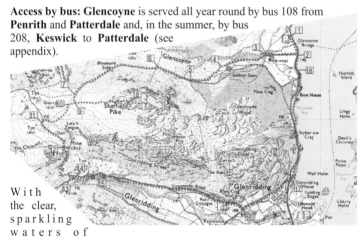

With the clear, sparkling waters of **Ullswater** straight ahead, we turn right out of the car park (Wp.1 0M) to walk along the road to reach a farm track (Wp.2 3M).

Turning right here, we stroll up the surfaced track to **Glencoyne**, an attractive National Trust-owned farmhouse dating from 1629, nestled at the base of the fells. Yellow waymarkers indicate that we bear right through the farmyard to pass between the farmhouse on our left and an outbuilding on our right. At the corner of the farmhouse, markers send us left through a gate between the buildings (Wp.3 9M).

Glencoyne

Once through, we climb the grassy fellside on a faint path that quickly levels off.

Seldom Seen, Sheffield Pike behind

With **Glencoyne Beck** below us, we pass the isolated stone cottages of **Seldom Seen** on our left (18M). Having crossed two small tributary streams (sometimes dry in summer), we turn left at a yellow waymarker (Wp.4 21M) to head up to the drystone wall high above us. The going is good on the steep, faint path, as we plod straight up the grassy fellside, swinging right as we approach the wall.

Going through a gate (Wp.5 33M) at the top of some steps at a kink in the wall, we turn right. Climbing slowly but surely with the wall on our immediate right, frequent rest stops are justified by the views behind us. Turning round, we are looking straight down **Ullswater** towards **Cross Fell**, the highest point in the **Pennines**.

Once through a gate in a wall that cuts straight across our route (Wp.6 49M), we turn half-left as the waymarker indicates to climb slightly, passing a large, upright boulder on our right. The gradient eases, although the general direction is still 'up' as we cross the open fellside, heading towards **Glencoyne Head**. This isn't a particularly busy route on to the fells, so it's a good place to stop and savour the peace; the silence is broken only by the sound of rushing water in the valley bottom far below us.

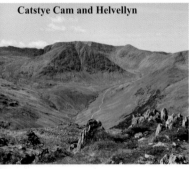
Catstye Cam and Helvellyn

Twenty minutes beyond the gate the slopes to our right steepen considerably and we swing SW on our approach to the pass at **Nick Head**. Turning left at the next fork (Wp.7 75M) - just before we actually reach the pass - we begin the final pull to the top of **Sheffield Pike**. As the path swings left (SE and then E), we get our first breathtaking view of **Helvellyn** with the pyramid-like **Catstye Cam** crouching in front of it.

The ground can be a little damp in places, but the gradient is relatively easy as we stride towards the summit, which is marked by a cairn (Wp.8 91M). Sitting next to the cairn is an unusual carved stone that looks a little like a headstone. Fear not! You're not eating your sandwiches on top of some poor soul's mortal remains; this is an 1830 boundary stone that divided the mining royalties of Hasell, of **Dalemain**, from those of Marshall, of **Patterdale Hall**. The view from the top - as from the top of every Lakeland fell - is magnificent, especially to the east where we are looking right down **Ullswater** to **Pooley Bridge** and the **Pennines** beyond. The long ridge in the middle ground to the SE is home to the Roman road, **High Street** (see picture on next page).

Retracing our steps, we head back down the fell towards the pass that we were approaching when we left the main path at Wp.7. We don't, however, go all the way back to Wp.7. Instead, as we approach the pass, we bear left at an indistinct fork (Wp.9 102M) to gain a clearer path at a T-junction (Wp.10 103M). Turning left, we thunder down the wet, grassy slope towards the ugly spoil heap below. As we approach the beck, we swing to the right to head for the footbridge at the base of the spoil slope. Crossing (Wp.11 112M), we pick up a cairned path between the spoil slopes and the beck, running almost parallel with the beck for a while (SE).

View from the top of Sheffield Pike

Happily turning our backs on this pile of mess left by the mines, we begin our descent towards **Glenridding**. Seven minutes beyond the bridge, we reach an area of horrendous erosion (Wp.12). Zigzagging its way down through this chaos, believe it or not, is our path. But things are not as bad as they seem - the Lake District National Park Authority (with financial help from the North West Development Agency and the Environment Agency) has spent many hundreds of thousands of pounds stabilising this fellside and trying to lessen the visual impact of the mining legacy. Beyond the notice asking walkers to stick to the waymarked path, things get a lot easier – our knees, in particular, welcome the gentle zigzags.

Although the notice at the top suggests there are many waymarkers guiding us down, there aren't. The first one appears 18 minutes into the descent from Wp.12 and indicates that we *must* turn right at this bend; the path straight ahead leads only to mine workings. We turn left at the next waymarker (Wp.13 139M) to drop down on to a clearer track (Wp.14 140M). Turning left, we slip-slide our way down this very loose, winding track to the buildings of **Greenside Mine**, now converted into hostels and outdoor pursuit centres.

Going through a gate (Wp.15 147M), we stride down the vehicle track to pass the youth hostel on our right. Passing several groups of cottages on our left, we eventually leave the surfaced track by turning left when the lane swings sharp right (Wp.16 169M). There's a sign on the left indicating that this public footpath will lead us to the lake. Going through a gate, we keep to the gravel track above the cottages of **Row Head** and, beyond the next gate, start losing height. (GPS reception is intermittent for the next 0.75 miles.) Dropping down to the main road on the outskirts of **Glenridding** (Wp.17 179M), we carefully cross over. For refreshments, turn right to detour into **Glenridding**, 0.3 miles away. Otherwise, we turn left along the roadside path.

When the roadside path ends just 100 yards after we join it, we drop down to the right to gain the lakeside path. Sadly, this isn't continuous and we soon find ourselves back on the road (185M). Still heading in the same direction, we walk along the road for two minutes and then pick up a narrow path running just below the road in the woods beside the lake. Regaining the road a little further on (Wp.18 191M) and with the lake still on our right, we stroll the 400 yards back to the car park.

Two wonderfully located tarns are visited on this straightforward walk - pretty **Lanty's Tarn**, just above **Glenridding**, and **Red Tarn**, spectacularly situated at the bottom of the cliffs of **Helvellyn's** east face and between the mountain's famous two *arêtes*, **Striding Edge** and **Swirral Edge**.

The route follows clear paths throughout, although it gets a little muddy near **Red Tarn**. The ascent is about 2½ miles long and, although fairly steep, does not involve any difficulties. The return route is via the old **Greenside Mines**.

3/4 | 3¼ H | 7½ miles/12km | 642m / 642m | 5

Access by car: The walk starts from the main car park in **Glenridding**, just off the A592. Unless you are staying in the village, you will need to drive to the start of the walk or use public transport (see below).

Access by bus or boat: Glenridding is served by the Ullswater Steamers as well as by bus 108 from **Penrith** to **Patterdale** and, during the summer, by the Kirkstone Rambler from **Bowness-on-Windermere** and the 208 between **Keswick** and **Patterdale** (see appendix).

Setting off from the National Park car park (Wp.1 0M), we turn right at the main entrance, then right again along a private road immediately after crossing **Glenridding Beck**. After we've gazed into the windows of a few shops and a couple of tea-rooms (just a few of the many places in which to eat in the village), the asphalt lane becomes a rough track as we stroll with the beck on our right.

Bearing left at a fork (Wp.2 6M) towards **Lanty's Tarn** and **Helvellyn**, we begin to climb, gently at first. Drawing level with an attractive cottage on our right, we pass through a gap in the fence on our left (Wp.3 10M) towards

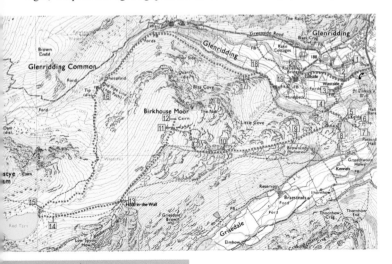

Lanty's Tarn and **Grisedale**. We soon link up with another path coming in from the right as we start climbing more steeply on a constructed path through pretty woods.

Going through a kissing gate (16M), we leave the trees and greet the bracken-covered slopes that replace them. In another two minutes we approach another gate (Wp.4 18M), but swing left instead of going through it to head straight up the fellside, still following signs for **Lanty's Tarn** and **Grisedale**. **Ullswater**, to our left as we ascend, looks as brilliant as ever.

The view from Keldas

The path drops slightly to a gate (Wp.5 21M), beyond which we can see **Lanty's Tarn**. But before heading that way, climbing the stile beside the gate just off to our left gives us access to a short detour to **Keldas** for a lovely view of **Ullswater**. Striding up the first incline, we bear right as we reach a group of four Scots pines (Wp.6 23M) to clamber the final 55 yards to the top of this rocky knoll (Wp.7).

Bearing in mind that we're on private land with just this one permissive path, we'll have to return to Wp.5 the way we came, after taking a rest and some photos.

Going through the gate at Wp.5, we come to the small but beautifully situated **Lanty's Tarn**.

Lanty's Tarn

Surrounded by tall trees, this spot is popular with picnicking families. **Lanty's Tarn** was named after Lancelot Dobson, whose family (who lived in a large mansion near **Grassthwaite Howe**) owned much of **Grisedale** in the 18th century. The tarn was later enlarged by the Marshall family, whose home was **Patterdale Hall**. They fished here and also stored ice from the tarn - in many feet of sawdust and straw - in an ice house for use in summer.

Just 115 yards beyond the gate and immediately after passing the edge of the small conifer plantation on our right, we leave the clear path by turning right along a faint, grassy trod (Wp.8 30M). Following the edge of the forest and then a wall, we ignore one ladder stile on our right and then turn a blind eye to a plain wooden stile beside a gate, choosing instead to cross the wall - and escape from this often soggy ground - via a stone stile to our right (Wp.9 38M). Turning left, we plod slowly up the grassy path with the impressive, long ridge of **St. Sunday Crag** to our left (see Walk 15).

As we gain height, we catch our first glimpse of our next objective, **Birkhouse Moor**, straight ahead. Although it only reaches a modest height of 712 metres, it looks pretty intimidating from here. Do we really have to climb <u>that</u>? But things aren't as bad as they look as we soon join a constructed path (Wp.10 58M) which makes our uphill progress a little easier.

If you're wondering why there's such a clear, wide and obviously popular track heading on to the little-known **Birkhouse Moor**, it's because most walkers making their way up here have more challenging summits than little old **Birkhouse Moor** in their sights - this is also one of the routes on to **Striding Edge**. As we swing away from the wall, there's an unusual sight to our right - the entire length of the curvaceous **Ullswater**. Normally only small sections of it are visible from the surrounding fells, but here it is in its entirety. A rare treat indeed!

For the sake of erosion control, we should stick with the main path on this ascent, resisting the temptation of a faint track off to the left. Cresting the hill as we get our first views west, we turn right along a faint grassy path (Wp.11 78M) for a short detour to the top of **Birkhouse Moor**. This gives us the opportunity to rest and admire the great views to the east - and also gives peak-baggers the chance to say, "Been there, done that". It's hard to miss the summit (Wp.12 80M); it's marked by a whopping, great cairn built from huge rocks. The obvious question is … why would anyone lug all those boulders on to this grassy felltop just to build a summit cairn? Is there some ancient mystery here? Answers on a postcard please…

Retracing our steps back to the main path at Wp.11, we turn right to continue our climb. Striding out along the delightful ridge with a wall on our left, we watch as a magnificent picture opens out ahead of us. That sharp, pointed summit to our right is **Catstye Cam** (890 metres), which used to be known as Catchedican or, "the ridge with a steep, wild-cat's path". And straight ahead is the *cirque* of the mighty **Helvellyn** (950 metres) with its famous *arêtes*, **Striding Edge** and **Swirral Edge,** cradling the as yet unseen **Red Tarn** in their protective arms.

Turning right (away from the wall) when we meet a ladder stile on our left (Wp.13 96M), we can see the many walkers strung out along **Striding Edge** as we follow the solid path that's been built across this desolate bog. As the ground gets muddier and rockier, you'll know we're approaching the bowl that houses the tarn. We must now turn left along a narrower path (Wp.14 107M) to get to the water's edge.

Mist descends over Red Tarn

At 718 metres, **Red Tarn** is the sixth highest tarn in the Lake District and is home to brown trout and the rare schelly. It can be an eerie place; with the dark crags of **Helvellyn** towering above us and the prevailing south-westerlies suddenly halted in their progress by the barrier thrown up by the mountains, an uneasy, almost ominous silence suddenly descends.

Once we've had our fill of the tarn, we need to get back to the main path. To do this, we must first find the outlet stream; there it is, just to our right. Turning right, with the stream on our left, we follow it until we hit the path.

Turning left, we cross the outlet stream and then turn right at the next junction (Wp.15 112M). We hurtle down this wide, mostly solid track, and, before we know it, we find ourselves back on a fairly level valley path. We cross **Red Tarn Beck**, our companion for the past 20 minutes, via a footbridge (Wp.16 144M).

Place Fell from the *leat* path

Sauntering along this easy track, the rushing waters below to our left belong to **Glenridding Beck**, a popular destination for groups of gill-scrambling schoolchildren. As we pass above the converted buildings of **Greenside Mine** (where GPS reception is temporarily lost), the views ahead down the valley suddenly open out to reveal **Place Fell** and **Ullswater**.

We ignore a grassy path off to the left and keep to the clear, level path following the line of a disused *leat* that once channelled water coming off the fells to **Greenside Mine**, where it was used to provide power. (Although still marked on OS maps in blue, it's now disused and dry.) We don't leave the line of the *leat* until a wall blocks our way ahead (Wp.17 171M). Turning left here, we pick our way down a rocky ditch to a T-junction (Wp.18 173M) to turn right along a pleasant, grassy track.

Crossing the next ladder stile, we drop to another T-junction (Wp.19 181M) to turn left. Bearing right as another path joins us from the left, we follow this track down to **Glenridding Beck**. Just before the bridge, we turn right towards the car park (Wp.20 186M). All that now stands between us and a refreshing drink in **Glenridding** is a lovely stroll along this woody, beckside path.

13 HELVELLYN FROM THIRLMERE

I'm going to resist the temptation to wax lyrical about **Helvellyn**. Any serious walker visiting the northern Lakes and not going up **Helvellyn** is missing out on a wonderful day out. It *is* a truly impressive mountain –both for those clambering on its many faces and for those viewing it from afar – but it's also a very, very popular mountain. If you want solitude, you won't find it here.

If all you're looking for is a quick up-and-down route to the top of England's third highest mountain, this is probably one of the best (and quietest). The ascent is via the steep path on to **Browncove Crags** (859 metres) and then continues towards **Lower Man** before reaching the 950-metre summit. The return is via **Birk Side** and then through the forests above **Thirlmere**.

4/5 | 3¾H | 6.6 miles/10.6km | 827m / 827m | 2

Access by car: The walk starts from the United Utilities **Swirls** car park beside **Thirlmere** (GR NY316168). This is six miles south of **Keswick** on the A591 and is on a regular bus service.

Access by bus: Bus 555 – see appendix.

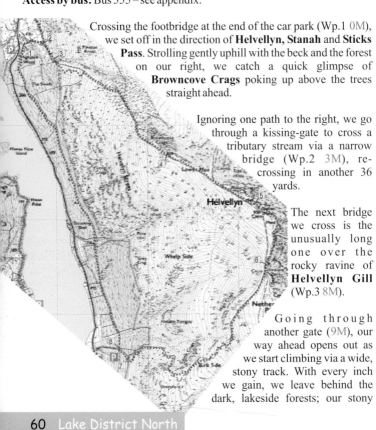

Crossing the footbridge at the end of the car park (Wp.1 0M), we set off in the direction of **Helvellyn, Stanah** and **Sticks Pass**. Strolling gently uphill with the beck and the forest on our right, we catch a quick glimpse of **Browncove Crags** poking up above the trees straight ahead.

Ignoring one path to the right, we go through a kissing-gate to cross a tributary stream via a narrow bridge (Wp.2 3M), re-crossing in another 36 yards.

The next bridge we cross is the unusually long one over the rocky ravine of **Helvellyn Gill** (Wp.3 8M).

Going through another gate (9M), our way ahead opens out as we start climbing via a wide, stony track. With every inch we gain, we leave behind the dark, lakeside forests; our stony track becoming a rock staircase zigzagging skyward. This constructed route makes our ascent easier, but it can make things a little dull.

Still, who can complain in such splendidly sylvan surroundings; the sparkling waters of **Thirlmere** lie below while **Skiddaw** dominates the northern horizon. The ridge on the other side of the reservoir is home to the desolate, boggy moors of Ullscarf (726 metres) and, as we gain height, some of the more westerly fells pop up from behind it – **Great Gable** is the first, then **Dale Head, Grasmoor** and, eventually, the **Scafell** group. It's a long, slow plod, but you'll love every puff and every pant of it!

Looking down Thirlmere

Thirty-five minutes beyond the last gate, we are joined on our uphill slog by a tumbledown old wall. The crumbling cliffs of **Browncove Crags** are straight ahead now, silently challenging us as our route curves around the western side of the fell – it's steep, but there's no scrambling involved. As the gradient eases, we stride out along the cairned track towards the summit, which is marked by a cairn to the left of the path (Wp.4 90M). Looking west from here, more peaks have joined the list we started compiling earlier – **Bow Fell, Crinkle Crags, Wetherlam** and the **Old Man of Coniston**, all on the far horizon.

We have an all-too-brief respite from climbing as the path dips and levels out for a measly two minutes and then our upward trend continues, albeit at a relatively easy angle. If you hadn't left all your worldly worries behind on the ascent, you are sure to lose them on this broad, open ridge as we make our way to the trig point on the summit of **Helvellyn** (Wp.5 114M). I could wax lyrical for hours about the top of this mountain, about how wonderful it is to just sit here, especially on a weekday when there are fewer people around, about the views in all directions, about those magnificent *arêtes*, about cool, blue **Red Tarn** below, about the crows doing their noisy acrobatics, about the great sense of being truly among the elements… but I won't.

Sticking to the eastern rim of the mountains and avoiding the wide path we came in on, it'll all soon become clear. Childlike, we inch ever closer to the edge, peering down on to **Striding Edge** and an assortment of impressive cliffs. All too soon though, the fun is over and, a third of a mile after the Charles Gough memorial (see Walk 14), we rejoin the main path (122M).

Striding Edge

We say our final farewell to the ridge proper in just 35 yards when the path forks (Wp.6) and we bear right. With the **Coniston** fells forming the horizon straight ahead, our descent is gentle at first, although the wide, stony path becomes steeper as we start to zigzag down the grassy slope.

Thirlmere from the top of Comb Crags

Reaching the top of **Comb Crags** (152M), we can see straight up **Thirlmere** to **Skiddaw**. Take some time to savour this beautiful scene because as we start inching our way slowly down the uneven stone staircase below us, there'll be few opportunities to look up from our feet.

But look up we must, or we'll miss this gorgeous natural amphitheatre that we're entering, where the calls of the ewes to their lambs ricochet off the craggy walls.

I'm not much of a fan of forest walking, but it's with a palpable sense of relief that we enter the woods (Wp.7 182M), knowing that the tiresome descent is almost at an end. As forests go, this one's not too bad – the trees are tall and relatively well spaced-out, so we can see the sky and even catch the odd glimpse of **Thirlmere** as we head downhill to reach a wide forest track (Wp.8 186M). Turning right through the gate towards **Swirls**, we begin the long walk back to the car park. (GPS reception is unreliable in this part of the forest and ceases altogether a little further on.)

Foxgloves in the forest

Having reached an open area and crossed two bridges in quick succession (201M), we go through a kissing-gate to follow a narrow path through a denser area of more interesting mixed woodland. Keep your eyes peeled for red squirrels here. A few years ago, these forests, owned by United Utilities, became the country's first red squirrel refuge. Conservation project NPI Red Alert North West hopes these adorable creatures, which have been wiped out in most of England and Wales, will be protected through the careful management of the woodland. It has installed rope bridges for the squirrels' safety and provided special food hoppers.

Emerging from the darkness 20 minutes later, we join another wide forest track to continue in the same direction as before. Nineteen minutes of dull plodding later and we arrive back at the car park where we started the walk.

If you're now in need of refreshments, the **King's Head Hotel** is just 0.6 miles north of the car park. Alternatively, if you head north along the main road for 150 yards and then cross over, you should find a small ice-cream van. He's normally there at busy times of the year.

The **Keppel Cove** track is one of the quieter routes up on to **Helvellyn** (950 metres) and, although it involves a fairly long walk in beside **Glenridding Beck**, it's also relatively easy. The great ridge walk from the summit - steep, craggy drops on one side; gentle, grassy slopes on the other - leads across the side of **Nethermost Pike** (884 metres) and **Dollywaggon Pike** (858 metres) before dropping steeply down to the atmospheric **Grisedale Tarn**. After the long walk in, we now have a long walk back via **Grisedale Beck**. After such a long day, you'll be glad of the wide range of good refreshments stops in **Glenridding** on your return.

From the top of the mountain, the only obvious escape routes back to **Glenridding** are along **Striding Edge** and **Swirral Edge**. Alternatively, if you need to make an emergency descent and using the *arêtes* is likely to prove dangerous, by bearing right instead of left at Wp.8, you can descend quickly to **Wythburn**, four miles north of **Grasmere** on the A591.

Access by car: The walk starts from the main car park in **Glenridding**, just off the A592. Unless you are staying in the village, you will need to drive to the start of the walk or use public transport (see below).

Access by bus or boat: Glenridding is served by the Ullswater Steamers as well as by bus 108 from **Penrith** to **Patterdale** and, during the summer, by the Kirkstone Rambler from **Bowness-on-Windermere** and the 208 between **Keswick** and **Patterdale** (see appendix).

Leaving the car park (Wp.1 0M) through its north-west pedestrian exit, we walk through the health centre car park and out on to a residential road to turn left (2M). Passing **The Travellers' Rest** (and making a mental note of its location for a beer stop at the end of the day), we swing right at a signpost (Wp.2 8M) towards **Greenside Mine** and **Keppel Cove** and then left at a postbox in the wall.

Striding out along this rough vehicle track, we pass several attractive cottages on our way up to the hostels and self-catering cottages that now occupy the site of the former **Greenside Mine** (30M). Lead mining started here in the seventeenth century, although serious development didn't begin until 1818. By 1849, there were 300 workers at **Greenside**, making it the largest lead mine in England. It was the first mine in Britain to use electrical winding and underground haulage, generating its own electricity by means of water turbines. The mine operated until 1962, producing about 2,400,000 tons of lead ore and 2 million ounces of silver during its lifetime. At one stage, it was leased to the Atomic Energy Authority who carried out non-nuclear explosions here to test seismic equipment.

Plodding uphill past the last of the **Greenside** buildings, we ignore the path off to the left to **Red Tarn** and **Helvellyn** (Wp.3) and instead follow signs for 'Brown Cove' and 'Whiteside Bank'. After wandering slowly uphill along

... the impressive peak of Catstye Cam ahead ...

this clear, wide, valley track with the impressive, pyramid-like peak of **Catstye Cam** (890 metres) ahead (see photo on the next page) and to our left, we bear right at an obvious fork (Wp.4 63M). Zigzagging our way slowly up th grassy fellside, our eyes are drawn time and time again to the gradually unfolding view of **Helvellyn** to our left.

The *arête* linking **Catstye Cam** and **Helvellyn** is **Swirral Edge**. The dam below us is one of many built for **Greenside Mine** and was responsible for one of the mine's most notable disasters; during a storm in 1927 it burst, devastating part of **Glenridding**, although luckily no one was killed.

Fifty minutes beyond the fork, as the path levels out briefly, we join another cairned track coming in from **Raise** (883 metres) to our right (Wp.5).

Now ambling along a lovely, wide ridge route, we can pick out **Skiddaw** and **Blencathra** to the north as the views open out. We make our way easily to the cairn marking the top of **Whiteside Bank** (863 metres, see picture on next page) from where the views include **Bow Fell** and the **Scafell** range to the south-west.

Having already climbed 710 metres, and

The top of Whiteside Bank

with 87 vertical metres still to go to the top of **Helvellyn**, it's with a heavy heart that we now drop down to a dip in the ridge. Trying to gain momentum, we thunder down this loose path and then shoot up the other side, gradually losing steam as we approach the top of **Lower Man** (925 metres). From its summit cairn (Wp.6 139M), we bear left for the final, easy pull to the top of **Helvellyn** itself (Wp.7 151M).

I won't even bother to list the mountains you can see from this wonderful spot – it's more a case of what fells *can't* you see. The top of England's third highest mountain is a broad plateau with grassy slopes running down to the west and steep cliffs and *arêtes* to the east.

The summit shelter on Helvellyn

The most interesting route across the top sticks to the eastern edge. This allows us to look down on to **Red Tarn** and the many brave souls strung out along **Striding Edge** and **Swirral Edge**, picking their way carefully along the steep-sided vertiginous ridges.

The exit from **Striding Edge** is marked by a plaque telling the story of Charles Gough, whose body was found in 1805 at the base of the crags beneath this spot. His rotting remains were guarded for three months by his dog, a story that inspired Sir Walter Scott to write the poem, 'Climbed the Dark Brow of

Mighty Helvellyn', and William Wordsworth to pen 'Fidelity'.

Leaving the crowds that inevitably pack the top of **Helvellyn** at all times of the year, we amble along the ridge in a southerly direction, bearing left at a distinct fork (Wp.8 155M).

Grisedale Tarn

Half an hour of delightful, undulating ridge path is followed by half an hour of knee-crunching descent as we slip-slide our way down the badly eroded, loose path on the south face of **Dollywaggon Pike**. This section is tiresome, but the calm, blue waters of beautiful **Grisedale Tarn** below will us on.

As the gradient eases off, we bear left away from the tarn and towards **Grisedale**, joining a path coming in from the right (Wp.9 220M). Sixty yards to the right of this junction is the **Brothers' Parting Stone**, where Wordsworth said a final farewell to his brother John. A few poignant lines commemorate the event.

Ruthwaite Lodge

Picking our way down into the valley along a stony path, we pass **Ruthwaite Lodge**, a former shooting hut that has been restored by Outward Bound Ullswater and is dedicated to two of its instructors killed on New Zealand's highest mountain, **Mount Cook**, in 1988.

Coming to a parting of the ways next to a small bridge (Wp.10 255M), we keep straight on, heading for a second bridge just 230 yards ahead. Crossing, and starting to feel the many miles behind us now, we amble slowly along the mostly level bridleway through the sheep-filled dale, bearing right when we reach a surfaced lane (Wp.11 298M). Once through a kissing-gate (Wp.12 303M), we ignore the track off to our left and keep straight ahead on a pleasant, woody lane until we reach the main road (Wp.13 313M). Turning left and with gorgeous **Ullswater** to our right, we stroll the 0.6 miles back to the car park in **Glenridding** (Wp.1) along roadside permitted paths.

This is the 'other' **Fairfield Horseshoe**, a totally different undertaking to the more popular route that starts from **Ambleside**. This one uses **Patterdale** as its base, climbing **St Sunday Crag** (841 metres) on the way up to the ever-popular **Fairfield** (873 metres). The return is via **Hart Crag** (822 metres) and then along the lonely ridge of **Hartsop above How**. I love this walk. I love the views from **St Sunday Crag**, I love the airy feel of the **Cofa Pike** ridge, I love looking down on the spectacular crags of **Fairfield**'s northern face and I love the ease of that final, grassy ridge.

There are some stiff climbs on the way up to **Fairfield** and some of the descents can be a little wearing, especially coming down the loose, rocky path from **Hart Crag**, but all the difficulties are worth it.

In the case of an emergency, it is possible to descend from **Deepdale Hause** (Wp.7). By turning right here, you descend to **Grisedale Tarn**, where you turn right again to follow **Grisedale Beck** back to **Patterdale**.

Access by car: The walk starts at the church in **Patterdale** (GR NY392161), 0.7 miles south of the centre of **Glenridding** village. There is parking to be had in **Patterdale.**

Access by bus: The village is served all year round by bus 108 from **Penrith** and, in the summer, by the Kirkstone Rambler between **Glenridding** and **Bowness-on-Windermere** and the 208 from **Keswick** (see appendix)

Standing with our backs to the church (Wp.1 0M), we turn left along the road (towards **Glenridding**) and then take the first road on the left (Wp.2 3M). (GPS reception is poor in this area.) With the high fells beckoning, we head up the winding, wooded road with purposeful strides, only leaving it when we reach a gate on our left with a footpath sign beside it (Wp.3 10M). Going through the gate, we march along the clear, wide track that leads to a locked metal gate (11M). Climbing the stile next to it, we ignore the clear track cutting straight across our route and instead head straight up the steep fellside path in a southerly direction.

Ullswater

The path is very badly eroded so it can be loose in places, although, at the time of writing, there were signs that the hardworking, often elusive 'path fairies' were about to start repairs. Coming to a wall with a stile (Wp.4 33M), the views to the south open out briefly. Crossing, we continue our slow plod up the fellside, taking time to stop and look behind at the ever improving view of **Ullswater**. After another 12 minutes of ascent, our way

Looking across to Striding Edge

ahead briefly eases, allowing us to enjoy the views across **Grisedale** to the **Helvellyn** range. Our path is mostly stony but it does have a tendency to vanish into thin air on boggy stretches, leaving us bewildered and stranded. Don't panic though! By keeping to a south-westerly direction, within 50 yards or less, the path magically reappears. Savour this brief respite from climbing, because the way ahead steepens considerably later. Bearing right at a fork (Wp.5 81M), we avoid the dull path that skirts around the side of the fell and head instead for the more interesting ridge path. "Interesting" because it's rocky - not exactly a scramble but not a dull plod either - and because it gives us a fantastic view of **Striding Edge**.

Before we know it the gradient eases, and we stride out along a wide, cairned path to the top of **St Sunday Crag**, known as **The Cape** (Wp.6 107M). The view east from here towards the **Pennines** is magnificent; and let's not forget about those wonderful, craggy mountains ahead.

Thundering along the next section of gently-descending, sometimes narrow ridge is pure delight, with the dark recesses of little-visited **Deepdale** to our left and, to our right, steep slopes leading down into **Grisedale**. These slopes consist of a mile-long series of crags, interspersed with gullies and an *arête*, **Pinnacle Ridge**, a favourite haunt of local climbers. Our way ahead starts climbing again after the pass at **Deepdale Hause** (Wp.7 130M) and there's an easy scramble to reach the exposed, airy ridge of **Cofa Pike** (Wp.8 162M), a great vantage point from which to admire **Fairfield**'s magnificent crags. Assuming you don't suffer from vertigo, it's a wonderful place to be. I once stood here and was able to look <u>down</u> on a RAF pilot negotiating the narrow gap between the mountains on the **Fairfield** side of **Grisedale** and the **Helvellyn** group on the other side. For those of a more nervous disposition, the trickiest section of ridge can be avoided by using a path just below the ridge to our right.

There's just time to catch your breath after this exhilarating scramble before the final climb on to **Fairfield**. This is very loose ground, so it can be difficult getting a foothold.

The summit (Wp.9 179M) is a wide, flat expanse, from where we get our first decent views to the west. The **Coniston** mountains, **Bow Fell, Scafell Pike, Great Gable, Grisedale Pike** – they're all there. And if we inch carefully over to **Fairfield's** north-eastern edge, we get to see some more of those dark, forbidding crags that we first spotted from **Cofa Pike**. If you stop for a bite to eat, you'll no doubt be approached by one of the pushy Herdwicks that frequent this felltop. For those used to sheep running away at the first sign of humans, it is quite disarming to suddenly be hassled for your sandwiches by a rather insistent ewe.

'Lambushed' on Fairfield

With so many cairns and shelters dotted about on the summit, it's easy to lose your bearings on **Fairfield**. Our path is the one heading off south-east, soon veering east. (If you miss it and head south-west by accident, you could end up in **Ambleside**, many, many miles from where we started!)

We drop to the *col* at **Link Hause** and then climb easily to **Hart Crag** (Wp.10 207M). The top is a jumble of angular boulders, the summit itself marked by a cairn. From the summit, we retrace our steps for 86 yards, until we come to a faint path to the right (Wp.11), the muddy junction marked by a cairn.

Turning right, we follow the cairns down on to a clear, rocky track. We pick our way carefully and then, when the path levels off briefly, watch for a faint path heading off down the grassy slope to our right (Wp.12 220M). This junction is also marked by a cairn. The more adventurous can stick to the main path, which heads down a steep, precipitous crag, but I prefer to bear right here and take my chances on the stony path that we're now heading down to. It is extremely loose underfoot, almost scree, but if you relax into it and let it carry you down, things get a lot easier. After this tiresome descent, we find ourselves on a delightfully long ridge, known as **Hartsop Above How**. Mostly grassy, sometimes peaty and occasionally craggy, it stretches on into the distance invitingly. We stride out with **St. Sunday Crag** towering over us to the left; the impressive rocky face to our right is **Dove Crag**. There's not a soul about - for some unknown reason, **Hartsop Above How** doesn't inspire the crowds, so you should have it practically to yourself. Up and down we go along the undulating ridge, sometimes having to detour around boggy stretches, sometimes having to lower ourselves gingerly down spiky crags.

Soon after passing (and ignoring) a ladder stile in the wall to our right, we snatch a quick glimpse of **Brothers Water** to our right. (If you're short you'll have to stand on tiptoe to see over the wall.) Regarded by some as one of the Lake District's smallest lakes and by others as one of its largest tarns, **Brothers Water** used to be known as Broad Water, but was renamed in the nineteenth century after two brothers drowned here. Dorothy Wordsworth referred to it as "the glittering, lively lake".

Where a wall blocks our further progress down the ridge, we cross it via a ladder stile (Wp.13 302M). As our grassy descent steepens, we are guided by a series of waymarker posts. Crossing a stile into some woods (Wp.14 320M), we descend a muddy path. (GPS reception is poor in the woods.) At the bottom, another stile gives us access to a small field, which we cross to a gate (Wp.15 327M). Going through, we turn left along the main road until we reach the driveway to **Deepdale Hall** on our left. We take the right turn immediately after this, along a public bridleway (Wp.16 332M).

Near the end of the day

Passing a pretty cottage on our left, we reach some gates at the end of the short lane. Going through the left-hand set, we cross several fields to come out on a rough lane along which we turn left (Wp.17 338M). We cross **Goldrill Beck** via a bridge, and climb to a junction of paths (Wp.18 339M) where we turn left towards **Patterdale**. Striding out along this lovely lane, we pass one set of buildings (uninhabited at the time of writing) and then, as we approach a second set, we have to cross a stile in the wall to our right (Wp.19 351M) to gain a permissive path around the back of the dwellings. Crossing over a bar in the wall just after a narrow bridge, we turn right as we regain the lane (Wp.20 354M).

Sauntering along now, we turn left at a T-junction (Wp.21 361M) to follow this asphalt lane to the main road, where we turn right (Wp.22 365M). It's a 600-yard stroll back to the church and our starting point (Wp.1), but we still have to run the gauntlet of **Patterdale** - can you resist the lure of cold drinks or the smell of food wafting from **The White Lion** pub and **The Patterdale Hotel**? Why bother to fight it?

16 LONGLANDS FELL & LOWTHWAITE FELL

The Northern Fells form one of the quietest areas of the Lakes; and the quietest area within the Northern Fells is found towards the west. So that's where we head now for a gentle stroll on two low-lying, grassy tops – **Longlands Fell** (483 metres) and **Lowthwaite Fell** (509 metres). There are no paths marked on the OS map for these fells, which probably explains why they are so peaceful, but there are obvious routes on the ground.

1/2 · 1½ H · 3½ miles/5.1km · 270m / 270m · 0

Access by car: The walk begins near the tiny hamlet of **Green Head** on the northern edge of the National Park (GR NY283367). From the village of **Caldbeck**, drive west along the B5299 for 2.9 miles until you see a sign pointing left to **Green Head, Fellside** and **Branthwaite**. Take this turning and, after a mile, turn right along a rough, dead-end track. The walk starts where, at a fork in the track, the main track bears right (0.3 miles from the road). There's space for a few cars here or you can park beside the road and walk up to the fork.

Leaving the main vehicle track, we bear left at the fork (Wp.1 0M) to head SW. Sauntering along this wide track, with a drainage ditch to our left, we soon cross the shallow ford at **Charleton Wath** (7M). Continuing along the track for a further 80 yards, we turn left at what at first looks like a reasonably clear vehicle track (Wp.2 9M).

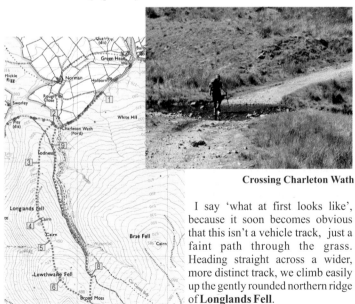

Crossing Charleton Wath

I say 'what at first looks like', because it soon becomes obvious that this isn't a vehicle track, just a faint path through the grass. Heading straight across a wider, more distinct track, we climb easily up the gently rounded northern ridge of **Longlands Fell**.

The gradient soon eases briefly and

we can see the Scottish hills and the **Isle of Man**. The small, oval-shaped body of water below and to our right is **Over Water**.

To its north-east is **Binsey** (447 metres), the most northerly summit in the Lake District.

As we join a track coming in from the right (Wp.3 20M), our way ahead steepens. But the climb is no hardship; the ground underfoot is grassy, buzzards wheel in the skies below us and there's nothing to break the silence of this remote corner of the National Park but the bleating of sheep, carried up on the breeze from the fields at the base of the fells.

Over Water & Binsey from Longlands Fell

Even this becomes fainter as we reach the top of **Longlands Fell**, marked by a cairn (Wp.4 33M). Now we catch our first glimpse of **Skiddaw** (SW). Dropping down into a boggy dip between the fells (Wp.5 38M), we bear right (SE) to start the climb on to **Lowthwaite Fell**, another short and relatively easy ascent on grass.

The top (Wp.6 46M) is marked by a small pile of stones, barely worthy of the name 'cairn', to the left of the path. Now the view of **Skiddaw** is even better, and we can also see the northern tip of **Bassenthwaite Lake**.

The path coming away from the top is not very clear, but we should be able to pick out the faint line through the grass descending SE and then gradually veering SSE. At the bottom of the slope, our way ahead becomes clearer again as we stride out across mostly level ground (ESE).

Reaching a small dip in the path just before it starts climbing again (Wp.7 54M), we turn left along a faint, grassy trod.

Wide open space of the Northern Fells

Strolling along this shallow depression in the fellside, the soggy ground to our left fills with wispy bog cotton (more commonly known as cotton grass) in the early summer. This isn't really a grass at all, but a type of sedge, the 'cotton' consisting of long white hairs that help the seeds to disperse in the wind. Cotton grass was once used for making candle wicks, stuffing pillows and even for dressing wounds.

Coming out on to a clearer track (Wp.8 58M), we turn left and almost immediately veer right to head gently downhill with the steep-sided gully of **Charleton Gill** (see picture on next page) on our right.

Charleton Gill

Having ambled happily down this track for 0.9 miles, we bear right along a very faint path that drops away from the main track (Wp.9 79M).

Heading across the grass (N) we drop down to the clear, wide track that we left at Wp.2. This is part of the 70-mile Cumbria Way (for further details, see Walk 22, 'River Derwent and around Castle Crag').

Turning right, we carefully re-cross **Charleton Wath** and retrace our steps to the start of the walk (Wp.1 90M).

Ewes and lambs near Green Head

Crouching at the base of the mighty **Skiddaw**, **Latrigg** (368 metres) is a grassy little hill that is very popular with visitors to **Keswick**. You are unlikely to experience any difficulties on this walk - it's a pleasant stroll on good paths with just one short climb; and there are great views on the way up and from the top.

The return route is along the disused **Cockermouth, Keswick and Penrith Railway**. This 31-mile line, built by Thomas Bouch, was opened in 1865, primarily to bring coke from the **Durham** coal mines to the iron-making industry on the west coast. Improvements in the making of coke from **West Cumberland** coal saw this traffic decline quickly after 1910. The western end of the line, together with the link from **Cockermouth** to **Workington**, was closed in 1966. The remaining section closed in 1972.

| 2 | 2½ H | 5.6 miles/9km | | 358m 358m | | 2 |

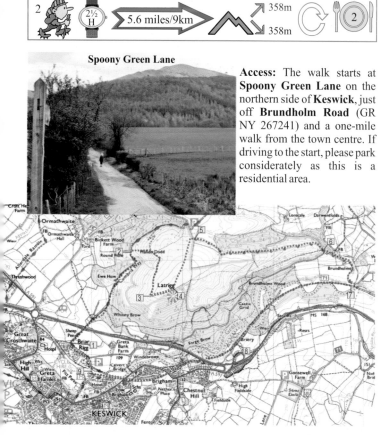

Spoony Green Lane

Access: The walk starts at **Spoony Green Lane** on the northern side of **Keswick**, just off **Brundholm Road** (GR NY 267241) and a one-mile walk from the town centre. If driving to the start, please park considerately as this is a residential area.

Heading straight up **Spoony Green Lane** (Wp.1 0M) towards **Skiddaw**, the senses are soon assaulted by the noise and fumes of heavy, fast-moving traffic as we cross the bridge over the busy A66. Having passed through a gate near a B&B (7M), we start making our way uphill on a wide lane, ignoring one turning off to the right signed 'Circular walk Brundholm Woods'. Joining another wide track coming in from the right, our path swings left and then right, the last swing culminating in a fork where we bear left.

The drone of the A66 gradually becomes a distant memory as our ears are filled now with birdsong. The mixed woodlands of **Latrigg** contain a rich variety of birdlife, as well as red squirrels, roe deer and badgers. As in many parts of Cumbria, foresters are encouraging natural re-growth of oak, ash, birch, hazel and other native species. Many non-native conifers are being felled, although some are allowed to remain because the red squirrels love the cones.

Just before reaching a fenced forest on our left, we turn right to head uphill on a grassy path through the bracken (Wp.2 25M). Plodding steeply upwards for nine minutes, we bear right as we meet a wider path coming in from the left. Breathing more easily now, we follow this mostly level path as it curves round the gully to a bench (Wp.3 45M). This is a great spot to rest and admire the fantastic views - over **Keswick** and **Derwentwater** and across to the fells of the **Coledale** and **Robinson** rounds - before swinging left for the last, easy bit of the climb.

The summit of **Latrigg** isn't marked. You'll only realise you're there when the path ahead drops slightly (Wp.4 50M). With no features of note, it's not a place to linger; instead, we stride out on the wide, grassy track that heads off to the left of the main path (NE).

Bouncing along on the springy turf, we must watch out for a stile to the right of the path as we descend towards the car park at the base of **Skiddaw**. We cross to it on uneven ground and use it to gain access to a wide, but muddy track on the other side of the fence/wall (Wp.5 58M).

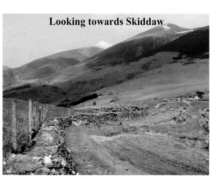

Looking towards Skiddaw

Turning right and trying to avoid the mud churned up by mountain bikers, we follow this track for almost a mile. Soon after joining it, we amble along with a forest on our left for company, but lose the security of the trees and the fence when they do a sharp left, leaving us to continue straight ahead on the easterly course we've been following for some minutes.

Dropping down to and through a gate (Wp.6 80M), we turn left and then immediately right. Bounding down this surfaced lane with the rushing waters of **Glenderaterra Beck** in the valley to our left, we reach a gate through which we turn right towards the next gate giving access to the railway footpath (Wp.7 91M).

Once on the old railway, we turn right. It's hard to go wrong now – this clear, wide, level track takes us all the way back to **Keswick**.

There's plenty of interest along the way. We are following the **River Greta**, crossing and re-crossing via several bridges. The river has been used for industrial purposes for more than six centuries. In the early 19th century it provided power for a pencil mill, several bobbin mills and a textile mill. We pass the site of an old mill (closed in 1961) near **Low Briery** (Wp.8 114M). This was known locally as the 'Fancy Bottoms Mill' because it made the intricate edgings for waistcoats.

By the mid-19th century, there were 120 water-powered bobbin mills in the Lake District, producing about half the entire world textile industry's bobbins.

Striding out past **Low Briery** and its caravan site, we reach the beginning of a boardwalk section as the path, temporarily abandoning the line of the railway, negotiates the increasingly steep-sided gorge (119M).

The boardwalk section

We pass under the massive A66 road bridge, pausing to note the plaque that informs us that in 1999 this monstrosity was awarded the surprising accolade of Best Concrete Engineering Structure of the Century.

The platform buildings of the old **Keswick Station** at the end of the path are now owned by the **Keswick Country House Hotel**, which is open to non-residents. Passing the platform and reaching the leisure centre's service road (Wp.9 141M), we turn right and then left at the small roundabout. Strolling along this quiet residential road for just over a third of a mile, we reach **Spoony Green Lane** and the start of the walk (Wp.1 150M).

18 HIGH PIKE

The secret to some of the most peaceful routes in the Lake District is to ask the locals where they head to on a sunny summer's afternoon when the rest of the National Park is packed full of hikers. Although it lies on the Cumbria Way, a long-distance trail from **Ulverston** in south Cumbria to **Carlisle** in the north, **High Pike** is still a relatively quiet fell – unless, of course, we happen to be up here on that sunny summer's afternoon when we're likely to encounter the occasional local exploring its many paths. **High Pike** also makes good winter walking when its rounded, grassy slopes offer a safer, easier alternative to their more spectacular southern neighbours.

This route approaches the 658 metre summit from the north, starting at **Fell Side,** a tiny, farming hamlet a couple of miles NW of the village of **Caldbeck**. Heading through the old mine workings of **Potts Gill**, the uphill sections are well spaced-out and the paths are mostly easy to follow, although they can be soggy in places. The descent, over **Deer Hills**, is a delight, especially late in the day when we might be treated to a stunning red sunset over west Cumbria.

Access: you'll need to drive to the start of the walk at **Fell Side** (GR NY303375), because the hamlet is not served by buses. From the village of **Caldbeck**, drive west along the B5299 for 2.9 miles until you see a sign pointing left to **Green Head, Fell Side** and **Branthwaite**. Take this turning and, after 2.2 miles, you will come to **Fell Side**. To reach the parking area, turn right up the farm lane opposite the phone box.

The concrete track leading to Little Fellside

We leave the parking area in **Fell Side** (Wp.1 0M) and head up the lane to a gate. Going through the gate and turning left, we soon cross a small stream. Ignoring the path heading uphill to the right 200 yards beyond the gate, we stay on the mostly level path until reaching a concrete track (Wp.2 8M) where we turn right.

We head towards the buildings of **Little Fellside**. A picture of rural tranquillity lies before us – pretty cottages dotted about, sheep grazing in the fields and the highest of the **Pennines** rising in the distance. It may not be typical Lake District scenery, but it's soothing on the soul nonetheless.

Just before the concrete track goes through a gate near an isolated cottage, we leave the track by turning right to walk just a few paces with a drystone wall nearby on our left and then bear right along a grassy path that is easy to miss (Wp.3 15M). The going underfoot now becomes decidedly soggy – a good chance to test how waterproof your boots are. But take heart – this is the dampest section of the entire day and the worst patches can be easily avoided.

The stream at Wp.4

Fording the stream (Wp.4 25M) we walk uphill for a few yards to the corner of a drystone wall on our left. We leave the clear, wide track here by turning right on to a grassy path (Wp.5) heading up the fell (ESE). It is important to take the path just <u>after</u> the corner of the wall, not the narrower one just <u>before</u> the wall.

At a junction with a clear track (Wp.6), we turn right to continue uphill. At the next junction (Wp.7), we turn right again along a gravel track.

Sheep grazing at Potts Gill

The disused workings we are walking through are part of the **Potts Gill** mine. Work started here in the 1870s, when prospectors unsuccessfully searched for lead and copper but found only *barytes*. Large-scale mining took off in the twentieth century when the market for this mineral

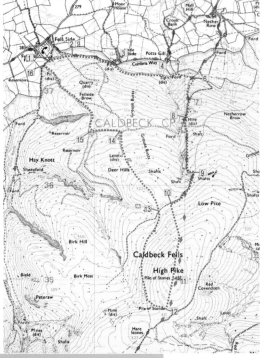

improved; the area was particularly busy during World War Two when *barytes* were needed for munitions. Operations ceased in 1966.

Just after passing a large, flat-topped mound on our left (the bulldozed remains of the mines), we leave the gravel track by bearing left along a grassy path (Wp.8 50M). We go straight across a crossroads with a wide, gravel track, and a few yards later, a grassy track joins our route from the right.

We stroll uphill until the next obvious crossroads with a grassy track (Wp.9 75M) where we turn right. Climbing more gently now our path swings SSW and then WSW. Just before our path starts dropping we see narrower paths off to the left and right (Wp.10 95M).

Turning left here, we head uphill (SSE) to pass a large stone shelter before arriving at the summit furniture of **High Pike** (Wp.11 110M), an impressive stone bench providing a welcome cool seat after the ascent. The views from here are extensive – **Blencathra** and **Skiddaw** ahead, the **Pennines** to the east and the **Solway Plain** and Scottish hills to the north.

The handy bench on top of High Pike

As we leave the top (SSW) there are two almost parallel paths heading down this slope. We take the right-hand path and at a crossing of paths (Wp.12), we turn right to head gently downhill (WNW). Our path now curves round the western side of **High Pike**, gradually losing height.

When we come to a clear, grassy track cutting across the one we're on (Wp.13 135M), we go straight across on to a narrow, level path across the top of **Deer Hills**. We descend gently on grass and then, when the path levels out again, bear left at the fork. It's not a problem if we miss the fork – whichever path we take, we soon reach a vehicle-wide track where we turn left (Wp.14 150M). This is time for really striding out – level walking on a grassy surface with some wonderful views of the west Cumbrian coast ahead. It's a satisfying way to (almost) end the day.

Our next turning is a little deceptive. It is important not to turn off this clear track until it ends at a T-junction (Wp.15). There is a fainter track continuing straight across, but we ignore this, turning right to head downhill. At a wide, gravel track we turn right again (Wp.16 170M) which brings us back to the gate above the **Fell Side** parking area and our start (Wp.1).

When you're tired of the rocky, stony paths of the classic Lakeland fells and need to feel grass under your boots, but you still want a good, long hike, **Knott** is ideal. This largely forgotten fell sits at 710 metres and has 'big' views in all directions - the Irish Sea, the **Isle of Man**, the Scottish hills, the **Pennines** and, of course, the Lakes. It's also a quiet spot - a great place to sit and do nothing for a while.

| 3 | 3¼ H | 7.1 miles/11.3km | ⛰ | 586m 586m | ↻ | 0 | 🍴 |

The start

Access by car: Drive to the start of the walk - a track (GR NY252337) 0.25 miles south of the hamlet of **Orthwaite**. **Orthwaite** can be found by driving north along the A591 from **Keswick** for 5 miles and then turning right along a minor road. There is room for three or four cars on the grass verge near the start of the track, but do not park in the passing places.

Starting at the public bridleway sign beside the road (Wp.1 0M), we head up the track towards **Burn Tod** and through the gate to gain access to a farm track. With views of the northern slopes of the **Skiddaw** range and **Dash Falls** (marked on OS maps as **Whitewater Dash**) straight ahead, we stroll along this track until we reach a public bridleway sign beside a grassy track off to the left (Wp.2 11M). Turning left, we plod gently up this delightful route, soaking up the peaceful atmosphere of these lonely hills.

As we gain height, you may catch glimpses of the white vein of quartz running through the rocks, a rare sight in the Lake District. Although you can't see it from here, the crag on which we are walking has a distinctive white band, almost like the white stripe running down a badger's face - hence the name, **Brockle Crag** (*brock* being the old English word for badger).

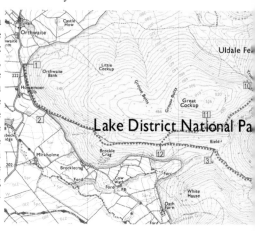

After 15 minutes of climbing fairly steeply, the gradient eases off, although

the general direction continues to be
uphill for a little while yet. Eventually we
drop down to a depression at the base of
several rounded fells, where we cross
Burntod Gill (Wp.3 43M).

As we plod away from the dip, with a beck
a little way off to our right, the path
narrows and becomes fainter in places.
There are some soggy sections, but
nothing too awful. The valley gradually
closes in around us until we leave the
grassy paths behind to ascend a steep-
sided gully on narrow and sometimes
loose, stony trods.

Having climbed for 20 minutes from Wp.3, we find ourselves right down in
the bottom of the gully with the beck close by on our right.

We cross the stream (Wp.4 66M) and then re-cross it three more times in quick
succession as we make our way upstream. After the fourth crossing, you'll see
a green, mossy gap in the gully wall up to our right. We exit the gully via this -
actually, we have little choice because the path in the valley bottom ends here.
Crossing the beck one final time (Wp.5 70M), we pick up the faint path to the
left of this mossy area, climbing gradually on this until we reach a T-junction
with a more obvious path (Wp.6 75M).

After the confinement of the gully, the views of **Blencathra** (straight ahead)
and **Great Calva** (the knobbly one up to the right) are very welcome. Turning
left, we trudge up the steep, grassy slope towards **Knott**. At the top of the
initial climb (90M), we are rewarded with our first decent views east to the
Pennines.

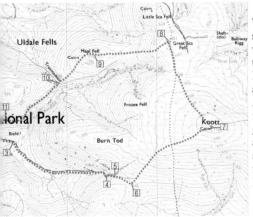

The gradient eases as we
stride out along this
wonderful felltop path
towards the summit of
Knott, which is marked by
a cairn (Wp.7 103M).
Although a generally
featureless top, this is a
great place to sit and relax
and soak up the
surroundings, far from the
madding crowds of the
Lake District honeypots.

There are several faint paths radiating out from the summit cairn. We want the
one that descends in a NW direction. Bounding along now, we drop down to a

boggy depression before climbing the easy slope to the cairn at the 651-metre top of **Great Sca Fell** (Wp.8 116M). Turning left, we take the right-hand of the two paths cutting faintly through the grass in front of us (WSW).

Descending from Great Sca

Thundering down the steep, western side of **Great Sca Fell**, surrounded by some of the most beautiful scenery that the Northern Fells have to offer, we quickly drop into a dip before the easy pull up to the small cairn marking the little visited 550-metre top of **Meal Fell** (Wp.9 132M). Choosing the right-hand of the two parallel paths that head away from the cairn in a westerly direction, 120 yards beyond the summit, we veer more to the SSW as we plunge down to a junction of paths in the pass known as **Trusmadoor**. Going straight across the first one, we head up the slope opposite to the three paths heading off to the left (Wp.10 148M).

Choosing the middle one, we keep left (on the level) when it splits in 53 yards. This route, although often only on sheep trods, keeps us well above a tricky scree section and also means that, when we get back to the more open slopes above **Hause Gill**, we can return a slightly different way to our outward route (although some repetition is still necessary).

Traversing the heathery fellside on a narrow trod, the beck below us to the left is **Burntod Gill**, which we crossed at Wp.3. Soon after the path starts swinging round to the west and immediately after crossing a rocky area - 0.4 miles beyond **Trusmadoor** - we bear left along an even fainter path (Wp.11 160M). Below us is the wide, grassy bridleway on which we started the walk.

Eventually, we need to rejoin that track, but for now we stick with the heathery slopes, a charming profusion of purple in autumn. We're on little more than sheep trods now, but as long as we always take the left-hand option whenever we come to a choice of routes ahead, we won't go wrong. Eventually, as promised, we drop back down to the clear bridleway (Wp.12 168M) where we turn right.

Heathery slopes above Hause Gill

Ambling along this level track, with **Bassenthwaite Lake** straight ahead, we pass the top of **Brockle Crag** just to our left before dropping down to the farm track at Wp.2 (184M). Turning right, the road is now just an 11-minute stroll away.

20 SKIDDAW, THE EASY WAY

At 931 metres, **Skiddaw** is England's fourth highest mountain. Yet this route, which starts at a height of 295 metres, is not particularly difficult. The first climb of the day up **Jenkin Hill** is fairly steep, but this gives way to a pleasant stroll up to the summit, from where we'll get superb views on a clear day.

It's a very popular route up the mountain, probably because of its relative ease. However, that's no reason for descending the same way - as most people tend to do. It's probably a sad lack of imagination that prevents these sheep-like walkers from striking away from the crowds and heading down 'back a Skidda'. This descent across open moorland may require some compass work for those without GPS, but it's a joy underfoot after having to slog up that constructed path earlier in the day.

It's probably best to avoid **Skiddaw** in windy weather when the top can get a little scary. A friend of mine was once lifted off his feet by a gust and then sent skidding across the icy summit. Only quick-thinking and his ice axe saved him from being blown over the edge.

Access: you'll need to drive to the start of the walk, which is the parking area (GR NY 280253), 1.9 miles north-east of the A66/A591 roundabout on the northern edge of **Keswick**.

Heading through the gate at the end of the parking area (Wp.1 0M), we turn left towards **Skiddaw, Bassenthwaite** and **Mosedale**.

The shepherds' memorial

Striding along with a wall/fence on our left, we keep left through the next gate (Wp.2 4M) to pass the memorial to the 19th century shepherds Edward Hawell and his son Joseph, breeders of prize Herdwick sheep. We amble along this pleasant, grassy platform for just two minutes, barely enough time to start enjoying ourselves before we begin the climb. Up and up and up the constructed path we plod. Seventeen minutes into the climb, there is a gate (Wp.3) - a good opportunity to stop and enjoy the amazing views behind us, especially across **Derwentwater**, before we head upwards again.

I have to confess that there is little to take our minds off the relentless slog other than the promise of the summit and the fact that, each time we turn around, the views have got even better than last time we looked. But take heart

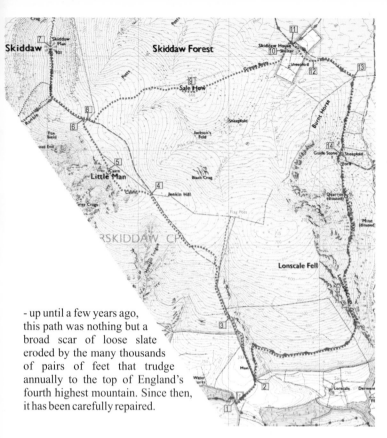

- up until a few years ago, this path was nothing but a broad scar of loose slate eroded by the many thousands of pairs of feet that trudge annually to the top of England's fourth highest mountain. Since then, it has been carefully repaired.

Having climbed for 35 minutes from the gate at Wp.3, the gradient eases slightly. Soon, we see the top of **Little Man** straight ahead. Reaching a gate in the fence at the base of **Little Man** (Wp.4 73M), we are greeted by a fine view of the rolling **Northern Fells**, uplifting after having seen little but the grey path at our feet for the last hour or so.

Ignoring the sign that tells us to go through the gate to get to **Skiddaw**'s summit - and ignoring our calf muscles that are begging to be allowed to walk that lovely, level path on the other side of the gate - we bear left to climb steeply up to **Little Man**. The first summit (84M) is marked by a tangled mess of metal fence posts. One more short pull from here brings us to the true summit, which stands at 865 metres (Wp.5 92M).

Plunging down the other side of this little bump on **Skiddaw**'s shoulder and then briefly following the line of a fence uphill, we rejoin the main path (Wp.6 102M) just above a gate in the fence; we return to this gate after having visited the summit.

Turning left, we start the final leg of the climb. It's not particularly hard going - in fact, after just seven minutes, we find ourselves on the broad summit, striding towards what can feel like the edge of the world after spending any time among the Lake District mountains. Effectively, the Lake District ends here.

Yes, there are the grassy, rounded tops of the **Northern Fells** off to the north-east, but the mountains proper end at **Skiddaw**'s trig point (Wp.7 118M). On a clear day, the views from the top are truly amazing - dozens of high peaks to the south and then, as we look north across the **Solway Firth**, some of southern Scotland's highest hills.

Sadly, we have to leave the top and head back down the way we've just come - but we only backtrack for a short distance. Still exhilarated from the visit to the summit, we thunder down to the gate (Wp.8 132M) just below Wp.6. Going through and waving goodbye to the crowds, 80 yards beyond the gate we strike out left (NE) across the grassy fellside.

There is a faint track on the ground, but it isn't easy to find. We can see it clearly on **Sale How** (666 metres), the small, rounded hill below us and slightly to the right. That's what we are now aiming for. We need to head in a north-east direction at first - walking parallel with the fence until it turns a sharp left after 100 yards - and then veer more east-north-east to pick up the track. This is lovely walking - wide, open, lonely fellsides with nothing to break the silence but the sweet singing of the skylarks. It's a wonderfully isolated area, a million miles away from that busy path that took us to the top of the mountain.

Lonscale Fell from Sale How

We squidge our way across a boggy dip before the short, easy climb up to the top of **Sale How** (Wp.9 152M), which isn't marked. Continuing on the now obvious track, we head downhill, aiming for **Skiddaw House** below us, hidden by a clump of trees – very conspicuous in an otherwise treeless landscape.

Reaching **Skiddaw House**'s boundary wall (Wp.10 170M) and keeping it on our right, we follow it round until we reach a wide track (Wp.11). Turning right to go through a gate, we pass in front of the building that, at 474 metres, used to be England's highest youth hostel.

It was built as a shooting lodge for **Cockermouth Castle** about 100 years ago and was then used as a shepherd's *bothy* until the 1950s. After a short spell as a schools' activity centre, the building was abandoned. In 1987 it was refurbished and turned into a youth hostel. Sadly, the YHA closed it in 2003 because of the resources needed to run such an isolated building. There are, after all, no mains services, no telephone or mobile phone coverage, and the only vehicle access is by tractor or quad bike. It's a lonely spot, that's for sure!

Leaving through the next gate, we keep the fence on our right to pass between two metal gate posts and then a gap in a wall. On reaching a clearer path (Wp.12 177M), we turn right to cross the footbridge over **Salehow Beck**. Strolling along this easy track across the heathery landscape, we soon reach and go through a gate (Wp.13 185M) beyond which we head in a SSW direction along a fainter path. The views ahead are of the fells above **Thirlmere**, framed by **Lonscale Fell** to our right and the western slopes of **Blencathra** to our left.

We bear right when the path forks (Wp.14 203M) near a group of ruined buildings below the pyramid-like peak of **Lonscale Fell**. Striding out across the eastern flank of the fell, we are accompanied by the noisy, rushing waters of **Glenderaterra Beck** far below to our left. There is a little ascent involved, but it's mostly a level path - and a delightful one at that.

View from Lonscale Fell's northern slopes

Having felt that we were at the edge of the Lake District earlier in the route, we now have a definite sense of walking back into the mountains. As the path hugs the increasingly craggy fellside, we begin to swing round to the SW and soon find ourselves on gentler and more sheep-friendly slopes (237M).

Dropping down slightly to ford **Whit Beck**, we then climb briefly to find ourselves back at a familiar gate (Wp.2 266M). Going through, we keep the fence/wall on our immediate right and retrace our steps to the car park (Wp.1).

21 A BLENCATHRA ROUND

Most people approach the mighty **Blencathra** (868 metres) from the A66, having been bewitched by its many magnificent arêtes as they've driven past on their way from the M6 to **Keswick**. Our route, however, tackles it from the east, starting and finishing on grassy tops - **Bowscale Fell** (702 metres) and **Souther Fell** (522 metres) - that are more typical of the Northern Fells than **Blencathra**.

We start from the pleasant fellside settlement of **Mungrisdale**. The initial climb is steep and the path is a little loose in places, but these difficulties are soon left behind as we stride out on the ridge towards the first summit. The crossing to **Blencathra** is often boggy and you could experience some difficulties in foggy conditions, so it's probably best to save this walk for a clear day. There's a short, sharp climb on to **Blencathra**, although we keep well clear of the technical difficulties associated with *arête*s such as **Sharp Edge**. Then it's down on to **Souther Fell**, probably one of the least visited tops in the Lakes. Maybe it's the story of the ghostly horsemen that puts people off!

In the case of an emergency, the best escape route is down the side of **The Tongue**. Having walked 400 yards from the shelter on **Bowscale Fell**, watch out for a narrow path through the grass to your left, easily identified by a solitary, small, upright stone a little way from the junction. Turn left here and it's an easy, 2-mile walk back to **Mungrisdale**. Also, just after Wp.14, instead of heading up on to **Souther Fell**, you can turn left, cross the **River Glenderamackin** and then turn right to walk the 2.2-mile valley path back to the village.

| 4/5 | 4½ H | 9.1 miles/14.6km | 907m / 907m | ↻ | 3 |

Access by car: The walk starts at the phone box in **Mungrisdale** (GR NY361303), which is signposted off the A66, seven miles east of **Keswick**. There is plenty of room for parking.

Access by bus: The village is served by the Caldbeck Rambler, an infrequent bus that runs daily during the school summer holidays but only on Saturdays during the winter (see appendix).

From the phone box (Wp.1 0M), we turn left along the road to wind our way through peaceful **Mungrisdale**. The church is one of many in north Cumbria dedicated to St. Kentigern, also known as Mungo. Bishop of Glasgow in the sixth century, he was later persecuted for his views and had to flee Scotland.

Mungrisdale

Immediately after passing a road to **Hutton Roof** on our right, we turn left along a rough lane (Wp.2 5M). Just 14 yards after going through a gate, we leave the track by turning right up the fellside (Wp.3 7M) on a faint, indistinct path. First we head to the left of the crag and then pick up a clearer line through the bracken. As we veer left, our way ahead gets steeper and looser, but despite the incline, it's best to shoot rapidly up this fellside; if you pause, you'll lose the precarious grip you've fought to maintain.

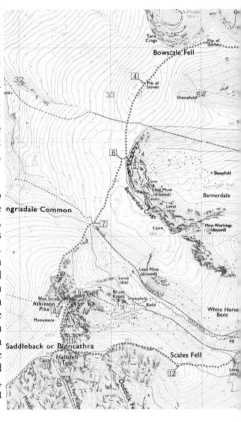

The hard work is over in no time; the path becomes grassier and the incline gentler after just 13 minutes. We are now able to savour the views as the pace slackens. The **Pennines** are to our right, but our eyes are drawn to the sylvan view to our left - **Souther Fell, Bannerdale Crags, The Tongue** and, just peeping above them, **Blencathra**.

Resisting the temptation to head off along one of the many sheep trods to the left, we keep to the main path as we plod relentlessly uphill. The tick-infested bracken gives way to heather and tasty bilberry as we gain height. Passing our first cairn of the day, we catch a glimpse of the top of **Bowscale Fell** in the distance; it still looks a long way off! To the north are **High Pike** (see Walk 18) and **Carrock Fell** (663 metres), home to an Iron Age hill fort sacked by the Romans.

Bowscale Tarn

You may have to divert around some of the boggiest patches of path, but in dry weather the ground is soft and springy, a delight to walk on. The route can be difficult to make out in fog, but there are cairns to guide us up the broad shoulder of the fell (W). When we get our first view of **Skiddaw** to the west, the path veers (WSW) as it dips slightly. This is a good opportunity to take a short detour to the edge of the fell to our right for a glimpse of **Bowscale Tarn**, one of the Lake District's most magnificent *corrie* tarns. The tarn is often used as a field study destination by local geography teachers trying to explain the processes associated with glaciation. It was also a popular destination in the nineteenth century, when Victorian ladies and gentlemen would make their way up hoping to catch sight of the two immortal giant carp - made famous in a Wordsworth poem - that were said to inhabit its dark waters.

Climbing out of the dip as we begin the final, easy pull on to the top of **Bowscale Fell** (SW), we find ourselves on a vehicle-wide track cutting through the grass and moss. The summit (Wp.4 91M) is marked by a cairn and just beyond it is a handy shelter in which we can rest out of the wind.

Leaving the summit after a breather, we head straight for brooding **Blencathra**. But what's that glinting on the fell ahead of us? Is that water? Yes, unfortunately, there's some very boggy ground ahead. In wet weather, it's best to keep left of it and then, as we approach the path that skirts the edge of the fell and winds round on to **Bannerdale Crags**, we turn right (Wp.5 103M). Picking our way across rough, damp ground, in 55 yards we pick up a faint path along which we bear left (Wp.6).

Dropping down to a pass (Wp.7 113M), we ignore paths off left and right and keep straight ahead to begin our slow slog on to **Blencathra**. Brave (some might say foolhardy) walkers might be seen edging along **Blencathra's** most famous and most notorious *arête*, **Sharp Edge**. More technical than **Striding Edge** on Helvellyn, this knife-edged ridge (it's not called "Sharp Edge" for nothing) culminates in a tricky scramble up **Foule Crag**, the oppressive cliff straight ahead of us.

The incline temporarily levels off as we reach a shelter to the right of the path (132M). The views south-west are opening out now and we can clearly see the mountains of **Coledale** (see Walk 31) through a gap in the fells.

The respite from the climb is short-lived as we labour up the steep, loose path on to the summit plateau. The top of the climb - but not the mountain - is

Looking down on Sharp Edge

marked by a cairn (Wp.8 140M). To get to the true summit, most people turn right here, but we head left, following the very edge of the fell and masochistically losing height so that we can look down on **Sharp Edge**. As we drop down to the narrow path around the edge of the fell (Wp.9 143M), there's a bird's eye view of the bare rock and all its horrors. If you're unsure of your footing (or your balance), don't stray too close to the edge.

Turning right, with views of **Scales Tarn** far below us, we stride out towards the summit. The top is marked by a cairn and, three yards to its left, is the site of the former trig point (Wp.10 152M). This is a wonderful place to be on a clear day. The *arêtes* leading up to the summit, the steep drops to the south and the mountain's relative isolation give **Blencathra** a very airy, exposed feel.

Looking south-west from the summit

Despite being so far north, you can see a lot of the major fell groupings from here. It's hard to tear oneself away from this fantastic vantage point, but to continue …

Retracing our steps for 150 yards, we bear right at a fork (Wp.11). The path fairies have been busy here. Not so long ago, this was a mess of ankle-twisting shattered rock and loose stones, not a pleasant way to descend. But the solid, well-constructed path that now zigzags down the fell makes things a lot easier and allows us to look up occasionally and enjoy the spectacular scenery.

Descent from Blencathra

With the steepest of the descent behind us, we stride out along a delightful grassy ridge with steep drops to our right. Just under 0.9 miles from the summit, we reluctantly tear ourselves away from this ridge by veering left at a faint fork (Wp.12 183M). I know, it's hard turning your back on one of the most impressive mountains in the Lakes, but it must be done.

Thundering down this mostly grassy slope, we go straight across the first clear path that we come to at the bottom (Wp.13 196M) and then, in two minutes, join a track coming in from the left. In another 200 yards (Wp.14 200M), we turn left, away from the main path, to begin the climb on to **Souther Fell** for a bit of ghost-hunting. We can see **Blencathra** again now - the gnarled and ancient **Foule Crag** looking positively evil from here.

This last climb of the day is a doddle compared with what's gone before. We soon reach the flat top and, as we come to a boggy area, bear left at a faint fork (Wp.15 214M) to visit a cairn on the western edge of **Souther Fell** (Wp.16 216M). It was on this top, on Midsummer Eve in 1735, that William Lancaster's servant saw a troop of ghostly horsemen crossing the fell. Exactly a year later, Mr Lancaster and his family saw the same sight. All were ridiculed when they told of the huge numbers involved, ascending a stretch of the fell that no rider would attempt. So, a few years later, again on Midsummer Eve, Mr Lancaster took 26 companions with him to witness the spectacle. They all saw the horsemen and even went to investigate the ground they had ridden on, finding no sign of hoof prints or other evidence that horses had passed that way. So, keep your eyes peeled!

To get to the true summit, we turn right at the cairn (ENE) along a faint path. Assuming we don't end up waist-deep in one of the well-hidden bogs up here (or get trampled by ghosts on horseback), in four minutes we regain the main path that we left at Wp.15. Another three minutes and we stroll casually past the easy-to-miss summit, marked only by a few rocks (Wp.17 225M).

Continuing north-east, we soon begin our steep descent. It's mostly on grass, although there are one or two rocky sections to negotiate. Standing immediately above **Mungrisdale**, our direct descent stops as we reach a post with a white waymarker on it (Wp.18 247M). Turning right as the arrow indicates, we walk along a narrow path through the bracken. I know! I know! We're heading <u>away</u> from **Mungrisdale**. And there's the pub, just a few hundred yards below us! But follow the signs.

The designated route descends to a fence corner (Wp.19 260M), where we turn left and then left at the road (Wp.20). Ambling along this country lane, it's now just under half a mile back to the phone box. We pass **The Mill Inn** on the way (good bar meals) and then turn left at a leafy road junction (Wp.21 269M) to find ourselves just 56 yards from where we started.

Mungrisdale

22 RIVER DERWENT & AROUND CASTLE CRAG

This really is a walk of two halves. We stroll through pleasant woodland and beside the **River Derwent** for the first half and then come back across open fellside above **Borrowdale** for the second half. Although little height is gained, the views as we climb **Broadslack Gill** on the western side of **Castle Crag** are superb.

Access by car: you can drive to the start of the walk – the National Trust car park in **Seatoller** on the B5289 **Borrowdale** road (GR NY245138), seven miles south of **Keswick**.

Access by bus: Seatoller is served all year by bus 79, the Borrowdale Rambler, from **Keswick**. In the summer, the 77/77A (Honister Rambler) also passes through the village on its circular route between **Keswick** and **Buttermere** (see appendix).

Heading for the far corner of the car park (Wp.1 0M), we stride up the broad track to go through the gate at the top.

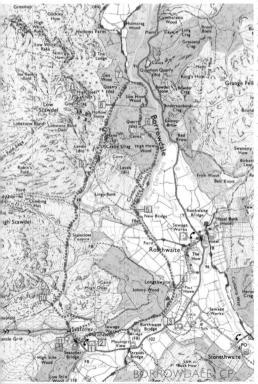

Bearing right beyond the gate, we stay on the level, right-hand path at the fork (Wp.2 3M) until we reach a pedestrian gate in the wall on our right (5M). Going through, we bear left to keep the wall on our left as we stroll through this pretty mixed woodland. (GPS reception is intermittent in the woods.)

If you're lucky, you may hear the sound of the **Borrowdale** cuckoo. Legend has it that the good people of this valley once built a wall across their beautiful dale to keep the cuckoo in so that spring would last forever. When the bird inevitably flew over the barricade, one of the dalesmen cried: "By gow! If we'd nobbut laid another line o' stanes atop, we'd a copped 'im!" This is supposedly why the dialect word for cuckoo - '*gowk*' - also means 'fool'.

The path seems to end abruptly when we reach a crag at the river's edge (Wp.3 16M). However, looking to our left, we see that the rocky outcrop can be easily negotiated via a few steps and crevasses. There is even a metal chain to hold on to for those who are unsure of their footing.

Back on surer ground, we confidently stride past the front of **Borrowdale Youth Hostel** to head down the drive towards the humpback bridge over the river. Ignoring it, we bear left (Wp.4 23M) along the rough track towards **Grange**. Passing in front of an old farmhouse, we go through a small gate beside the river to gain a narrow path.

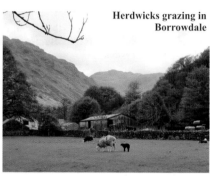

Herdwicks grazing in Borrowdale

As we amble along with the gently flowing **Derwent** on our right and the Herdwick-filled fields on our left, the craggy slopes towering over us and the sheep belong to **High Spy**, part of a wonderful ridge route that we undertake in Walk 30.

Soon after passing another humpback bridge on our right, we come to a choice of gates (Wp.5 39M). Deciding on the right-hand one, we have the river for company for the next 250 yards, then say a temporary farewell to it as the path veers to the left. But we're never too far apart - we catch glimpses of its sparkling waters as we meander through the woods at the base of **Castle Crag**. (GPS reception is poor in these woods.)

We're currently treading the **Cumbria Way**, one of two long-distance routes that we encounter on this walk. This popular, 70-mile path runs from **Ulverston** in the south of the county to the historic city of **Carlisle** in the north via **Coniston**, **Langdale**, **Borrowdale**, **Derwentwater** and the **Northern Fells**. Later in the walk, as we traverse the fellside above **Borrowdale**, we follow in the footsteps of long-distance hikers on the Allerdale Ramble. This 54-mile route starts in **Borrowdale** and then heads up towards **Skiddaw** before reaching the coast on the **Solway Firth** and joining the **Cumbria Coastal Way** as far as **Grune Point**.

Having passed some quarry workings and a spoil heap (54M), we bear right at a fork in the path (Wp.6 56M), heading uphill to a junction of paths at a signpost. Turning right towards **Grange**, we climb very briefly and then quickly lose what little height we've gained to rejoin the river (63M).

Turning left at a footpath sign just above a bridge over a tributary beck (Wp.7 70M), we head towards **Honister** and **Seatoller**. The beck is on our right at first, but we then cross it via a narrow plank bridge. Climbing gently, we leave the woods via a gate (Wp.8 79M) that gives us access to open fellside.

With the steep, boulder-strewn slopes leading up to **High Spy** on our right and the spiky, tree-covered summit of **Castle Crag** to our left, we plod slowly up the loose, stony bridleway for 15 minutes.

It's not a particularly steep climb, but it's worth stopping occasionally to turn around and enjoy the fantastic views of **Derwentwater** and **Skiddaw** behind us. **Castle Crag** is crowned by the remains of an Iron Age hill fort. The Romans also used it, probably taking advantage of its prominent, strategic position within the valley.

But the crag has been occupied more recently than that. Between the two world wars, two of the crag's caves became the summer home of Millican Dalton. Sick of being a commuter in southern England, he migrated north to the Lake District on an annual basis, making ends meet by leading walking parties on the fells and making tents and rucksacks. He turned one cave into a living area and one into a bedroom, which he called 'The Attic'.

Bridge over Tongue Gill

At the top of the pass, we are rewarded with views of **Borrowdale** and its many craggy mountains. Having walked just 160 yards beyond the pass, we have to leave the broad, level path at a cairn near a small waymarker (Wp.9 94M). Turning left, we head briefly downhill on a narrow path to ford two streams and then cross **Tongue Gill** via a double bridge.

Contouring around this lovely, grassy fellside above **Borrowdale**, we cross several streams (two via bridges) and go through several gates, only reluctantly abandoning our seemingly lofty position (in reality never higher than 245 metres) when we reach two gates next to each other (Wp.10 121M). Choosing the left-hand one, we plummet down the grassy slope in a south-east direction, turning left at the broad track.

Descending towards **Seatoller** in a rather roundabout fashion, we reach the road just above the hamlet (Wp.11 133M). Turning left and watching carefully for traffic on this windy section of road, we stroll the 160 yards back to the car park, which is on our left just after the last building.

There's plenty of variety on this walk. We start with an easy stroll along the shores of **Derwentwater** with its stunning views down **Borrowdale** and across to the **Derwent Fells**, which include **Cat Bells**. We then climb to **Ashness Bridge**, one of the most photographed places in the whole of the Lake District. From here, we gently ascend **Walla Crag** (379 metres) for some magnificent views before heading back down to **Keswick** on grassy paths and through attractive woodland. Apart from one short, steep section, all the climbs are relatively easy and well spaced-out.

2/3 | 3¼ H | 6.4 miles/10.2km | 405m / 405m | 5

Derwent Isle

The island just off the shore is **Derwent Isle**, the most northerly of **Derwentwater's** islands. It was once home to a group of German miners fleeing from the people of **Keswick**. They were employed by the Company of Mines Royal, which, in 1564, acquired a royal decree to mine and smelt in England, but they were forced to leave after several of them were murdered by local people. In 1778, the island passed into the hands of Joseph Pocklington. Apart from building a villa, Pocklington also constructed a number of follies on the island, including Fort Joseph. This was used during the Derwentwater Regatta, the centrepiece of which was a mock battle where local teams would attempt to land boats on the island and storm the fort's supply of beef and beer while avoiding fire from Pocklington's cannon. **Derwent Isle** is now owned by the National Trust and is the only inhabited island on the lake.

Access: the walk starts at the **Theatre By The Lake** in **Keswick** (GR NY264228). There's a car park beside the theatre or, if you are staying in **Keswick**, it's within easy walking distance of the town centre, where there is a large selection of good pubs, cafés and restaurants.

Striding down to **Derwentwater** from the theatre (Wp.1 0M), we join the crowds milling around by the lakeside, enjoying some of the most famous views in the Lake District. As we amble along the lane beside the lake, it's easy to see why it's so popular. There are stunning views across the water to **Grisedale Pike**, **Causey Pike** and **Cat Bells**. (GPS reception is intermittent in the woods around Derwentwater.)

Derwentwater

Keeping straight ahead when the path forks (8M), we stroll to the end of **Friar's Crag** for more great views down the lake, this time straight into the **Jaws of Borrowdale**. **Friar's Crag** was bought in 1921 by the National Trust as a memorial to Canon Rawnsley (1851-1920), a founder of the national conservation charity. Coming back round the crag, we walk down steps and

turn right at a level path (Wp.2 11M) to go through a gate. Wending our way along the 'lakeside' path, sometimes more lakeside than others, we pass through several gates, cross a small bridge and stroll through woodland. Exiting the woodland at a gate (Wp.3 22M), we turn right along a rough lane. We catch our first decent sighting of **Walla Crag** here - it's the heavily wooded lump of rock up to our left.

Having passed a superbly located cottage on our right (just imagine the views!), we cross a cattle grid and veer right. Bearing left when the gravel track forks (Wp.4 27M), we find ourselves back at the water's edge. The island straight ahead is **Lord's Island**, so-called because it once belonged to the Earls of Derwentwater. The remains of the manor house can still be seen on it.

Crossing another small bridge, we are now able to amble along the shore proper - a chance, perhaps, to dip your toes in the lake, but only in the hottest of summers. We enter woodland and then come back out into the open after another bridge. Seventy yards beyond this bridge, as we see the crags ahead of us coming right down to the water's edge, we have to leave the lake (Wp.5 43M). Using a faint path to our left, we clamber up the crag and, once at the top, turn right. Walking along the roadside path for just 4 yards, we cross the road to climb over a stile in the wall (Wp.6 45M).

Having briefly climbed steeply through a jumble of large boulders, we bear half right and ascend at an easier angle to a T-junction with a clearer path at the base of the impressive-looking **Falcon Crag** (Wp.7 50M). Turning right, we saunter along this mostly level path, high above **Derwentwater** and with the spiky crag towering over us intimidatingly, until we reach a cairn and signpost marking a fork in the path (Wp.8 60M). Choosing the higher, left-hand route, we stride out towards **Ashness Bridge**, climbing very gradually.

Once through a gate in a drystone wall (73M), we drop down, camera at the ready, to the road (Wp.9) near **Ashness Bridge**. Our route doesn't actually cross the bridge, but we will, no doubt, want to get to the other side to take a picture of the bridge with **Skiddaw** behind it –the classic image of **Ashness Bridge**, as seen on the front of many a chocolate box. (See photo on the following page.)

Ashness Bridge

Back on track, if we go back to where our route dropped down to the road (Wp.9), we will be able to pick up a faint path heading uphill (SE) with the beck on our right. Crossing a stile, we continue uphill in the same direction until we hit a T-junction with a clear track (Wp.10 79M). Turning left, we plod up to and through the next gate (Wp.11 83M).

Derwentwater, hardly ever out of view on this walk, is far below us as we now climb at a relatively easy angle across the open fell towards **Walla Crag**.

Looking towards Borrowdale

Reaching a stile in a wall (Wp.12 117M), we cross for the final pull up to the top of the crag (Wp.13 121M). The views from the top are amazing. Looking from the left, we see **Borrowdale** in all its splendour, **Derwentwater** (of course!) below us, **Bassenthwaite Lake** (beyond that is **Criffel** in **Dumfries & Galloway**), **Skiddaw** and **Blencathra**.

Keeping some of that vista in sight for just a little longer, we come away from the top in a NE direction to follow a path that skirts the edge of the crag for 120 yards and then drops to a kissing-gate (Wp.14).

Skiddaw

Going through, we turn left along a wide, grassy path. Soon with the wall accompanying us on our left, we plunge down into the valley that hides **Brockle Beck** and through a gate (136M) to gain access to a clear track. Ignoring a track off to the right after 110 yards, we drop down to a narrow bridge (Wp.15 142M).

Crossing the beck here, we turn left along the surfaced lane for 200 yards until we reach a small gate on our left (Wp.16), set back from the road and hidden by a wall and shrubs, so we need to watch carefully for it.

Once through, we descend the few steps to re-cross **Brockle Beck** via another narrow footbridge. Turning right, we head downstream, ignoring a left-turning towards **Great Wood** and **Borrowdale** after 270 yards.

Bluebell woods

Sadly, those magnificent views that have kept us enthralled practically all day are now briefly marred by a radio mast just off to the left. Passing underneath this metal contraption and heading into the woods, we do a sharp right turn to meet up with a track coming in from the right (Wp.17 157M). Bearing left along it, we stroll downstream through pretty woodland, a delight at most times of the year, but particularly wonderful in spring when the ground is carpeted with bluebells. (GPS reception is poor in the woods.)

Reaching a road on the edge of **Keswick** (Wp.18 163M), we keep straight ahead, passing several nice-looking villas. Turning left at a narrow track (Wp.19 172M) towards **Castlehead** and **Lake Road**, we stride out towards the trees. Going through a gate to enter the woods, we bear right after climbing the few steps and then left at a fork. (GPS reception is poor in the woods.)

We climb gently among the trees and then drop down to the **Borrowdale** road (Wp.20), where we cross over to turn left along the footpath. Turning right at the next signpost (Wp.21 185M), we stroll towards yet another area of woodland. (GPS reception is poor in these woods too.) Once under the shade of the trees again (Wp.22), we turn right and then right again at the next fork to amble back to the car park beside the theatre. The building itself, and our starting point (Wp.1 195M), are just off to our left.

If Walk 22 was a walk of two halves, this one is a walk of four quarters. We start with a short climb through woodland, which brings us to lovely **Watendlath Beck**. Next stop is the pretty settlement of **Watendlath**, the setting for Hugh Walpole's 1931 novel 'Judith Paris' and, in 1978, the last place in the Lakes to get mains electricity. This is a good place to stop and relax for a while (and maybe get a drink if the teashop is open) before setting out on the popular path up and over towards **Rosthwaite**.

But we don't go all the way to **Rosthwaite**. Instead, we leave the crowds to climb on to **Grange Fell** where we visit the peaceful tops of **Jopplety How** (400 metres) and **King's How** (392 metres). If you expect all the fells above **Borrowdale** to be heaving with walkers, think again! When I first explored **Grange Fell**, it was Easter and I expected the paths to be packed with families enjoying the school holidays. Instead, I found a secret place with not a single soul in sight. Kind Edward VII's sister Louise must have had this in mind when, in 1910, she dedicated the fell to her brother's memory "as a sanctuary of rest and peace". We see the memorial plaque soon after we begin our descent from **King's How** .

Access by car: The walk starts from the parking area (GR NY 256176) on the B5289 **Borrowdale** road, 0.25 miles north of **Grange** (3.6 miles south of **Keswick**).

Access by bus: The B5289 through **Borrowdale** is served all year by bus 79, the Borrowdale Rambler, between **Keswick** and **Seatoller**. In the summer, the 77/77A (Honister Rambler) also passes through Borrowdale on its circular route between **Keswick** and **Buttermere** (see appendix).

Turning right out of the parking area (Wp.1 0M), we walk along the road, passing several hotels and guesthouses. Soon after the largest of these, the **Borrowdale Hotel**, and just before we reach **High Lodore Farm**, we turn right at a footpath sign (Wp.2 10M). The gravel vehicle track leads us around the back of the old farmhouse where we pick up a footpath to our right heading up the hill into woodland. (GPS reception is intermittent in the woods.)

As this winds round, ensure you're not tempted by the track off to our left (13M); instead we swing right to pass a bench on our right.

Bearing left at a fork (Wp.3 15M), we trudge up to the next path junction, at which we turn left (16M). Upwards we plod, as the trees start to thin out, until we reach a wall. Going through the right-hand gap (Wp.4 22M), we keep straight ahead, down a grassy slope and then heading gently uphill on a narrow, stony path with the rushing beck on our left; this later becomes **Lodore Falls**, a rather disappointing cascade in anything but the wettest of weather. Just as we reach the side of the beck, there is a wonderful view downstream towards **Skiddaw**, best in winter when the trees are bare.

Going through a gate beside a churning waterfall (23M), we stick with the main path beyond, keeping right at the next fork (25M), then bearing right as we reach a rocky track coming in from the left. Beyond the next kissing-gate, we join a clear, dry track beside a footbridge over **Watendlath Beck** (Wp.5 31M). Turning right, we stride out along this mostly level path with the beck on our left.

Watendlath Beck

This delightful dale (225 metres above sea level), is one of **Borrowdale's** many hanging valleys. 'Hanging' above the level of the glaciated valley floor (**Borrowdale**), it was gouged out by a tributary to the main glacier, and so didn't erode as deeply. The difference in levels is exaggerated by the Skiddaw Slates of the main valley being eroded more quickly than the Borrowdale Volcanics, on which the beck lies.

The bridge into Watendlath

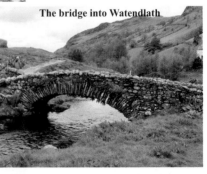

On reaching the bridge giving access to **Watendlath** hamlet (Wp.6 72M), our route continues straight ahead, ignoring the bridge. However, the popular National Trust-protected hamlet is worth a detour if only for the teashop serving up cakes and drinks from Good Friday until Halloween.

Watendlath was the setting for Hugh Walpole's 1931 novel 'Judith Paris'. It was the second of his four novels belonging to the Herries Chronicle. Set in **Keswick, Borrowdale, Watendlath, Uldale** and **Ireby**, these books told the story of Cumberland's Herries family from the 18th century to the depression of the 1930s.

Back on the main route, we stroll with the water on our left to pass through a gate and reach a fork (Wp.7 73M) where we turn right. Plodding uphill for seven minutes, we reach a relatively flat, high-level path with surprisingly good views down **Borrowdale** to **Honister**. I say surprising, as it seems that it was only a few minutes ago that we were walking along the valley, but, of course that valley was already at 225 metres; now we're at 320 metres.

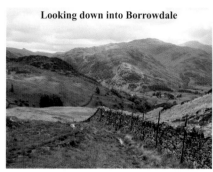
Looking down into Borrowdale

Exactly 0.45 miles beyond the bridge into **Watendlath**, and just after fording a small stream, we say goodbye to the beaten track by turning right along a very faint path (not marked on maps) heading up the grassy fell (Wp.8 85M). Squelching our way across some soggy ground towards a wall, we have ever-improving views of **Borrowdale** ahead.

We veer right as we approach the wall, ignoring a ladder stile to our left and climbing more steeply beyond it. Crossing the next ladder stile (Wp.9 100M), we bear left along the path through the heather. Despite being just a few hundred metres above some of the most visited areas of the Lake District, this is a very secluded spot.

After crossing another damp patch, our way ahead gets considerably steeper as we struggle up the last few yards to **Jopplety How**. Reaching a T-junction at the top of the main climb (Wp.10 106M), we turn right to scramble the final 14 yards to the summit for some great views of **Skiddaw** and **Derwentwater**. The top looks like a jumble of rocks, but it actually hides a lovely, flat, grassy area – a perfect, well-sheltered spot for a picnic.

Retracing our steps to the junction at Wp.10, we keep straight ahead to wind our way between the rocky outcrops that thrust up through this otherwise heathery fellside. Descending to a T-junction (Wp.11 118M), we turn right with views of **Skiddaw** ahead; **King's How**, our next target, is the knobbly top to our left.

Easing our way down the next damp, sometimes slippery slope, we cross a ladder stile and then stride out along a mostly level path to a stile in a fence at the base of some crags (Wp.12 125M). Crossing, we turn half-left (SW) to clamber up a grassy gap between the crags. Just beyond this first rise , we bear right at a fork (Wp.13 128M) to join a track coming in from the left. Trudging straight up the fell, we are rewarded at the top (Wp.14 136M) with a wonderful, uninterrupted view of **Skiddaw** and the whole of **Derwentwater**.

Uninterrupted views from King's How

To the right of the **Skiddaw** massif is **Blencathra**; and, further to our right, the long, notched ridge on the horizon belongs to the **Helvellyn** range.

The plaque to King Edward VII

Coming away from the summit cairn (NNW) we soon swing round (E) as we begin our meandering descent. Passing the plaque to King Edward VII on our right, we ignore a right turn at a cairn and instead follow the path as it swings round to the north-west.

With the ground underfoot rocky - and sometimes slippery after rain - the descent can be a little tiresome. Even when we reach the lower, wooded slopes and find ourselves on a constructed path, things don't get much better - the stones are often mossy. As we pick our way gingerly downhill, there is, however, one consolation; whenever we dare to look up from the uneven, slippery ground beneath our feet, **Derwentwater** shimmers ahead of us and, beyond that, is the mighty, omnipresent **Skiddaw**.

After 35 minutes of snail-slow descent, we breathe a sigh of relief as the gradient eases (just a little). Leaving the main path by turning right on to a faint path (Wp.15 175M), we drop down to cross a stile. (GPS reception is intermittent in this part of the woods.) Keeping the stream on our right and ignoring a path off to the left after two minutes, we amble down through pretty woodland to an open area at the base of the fells. Going through a gate near a house (Wp.16 192M), we gain a lane and stroll along this back to the B5289. Turning left when we reach the main road, the parking area is literally just around the next bend.

25 GREAT GABLE

As with **Helvellyn**, **Great Gable** (899 metres) is a must in any serious fell-walker's itinerary for the northern Lakes. The top is little more than a boulder field, but the views are simply stunning - possibly the best in the whole of the Lake District.

We start at **Honister Pass**, which lies at 335 metres, giving us something of a head-start. The ascent is via **Grey Knotts** (697 metres) and **Brandreth** (715 metres), a lovely ridge walk. The final pull up from **Windy Gap** between **Green Gable** (801 metres) and its more famous neighbour is on a badly eroded path, where we might struggle to get either footing or secure handhold. Care is required! We return via much gentler paths.

Access by car: The walk starts from the National Trust car park at **Honister Pass** on the B5289, about 9 miles south-west of **Keswick**.

Access by bus: Honister Pass is served by the Honister Rambler circular bus route from Easter until the end of October (see appendix).

Our day starts as we head through the pedestrian gate at the far end of the car park (Wp.1 0M) and turn sharp left to cross the slate mine's yard to a stile in a fence (Wp.2 1M). Crossing, we head straight for the fence to our right and, without further ado, start the steep climb on to **Grey Knotts**.

Almost 20 minutes after leaving the car park, the constructed path that has been easing our way up the fell, moves away from the fence and leads us in between some rocks where we are faced with a single rock step, easy for people with long legs, but a bit of a struggle for us shorties. Using hands and knees, we negotiate this first hurdle, glad that the confined space shields our ungainly manoeuvres from the eyes of longer-legged walkers.

Continuing upwards, the views are improving all the time. The ridge on the far horizon to our left is the **Helvellyn** range. Behind us, the south-western face of **Dale Head** is scarred by old slate workings. **Honister** has been producing distinctive green slate for more than 350 years. Today, it is the only slate mine in England.

Dale Head

We keep the fence on our right, ignoring any stiles across it until another fence running perpendicular to it blocks our further progress. Now, we cross the stile on our right (Wp.3 54M) and turn left to follow the fence on our left up on to **Grey Knotts**. On reaching another stile (Wp.4 57M), we re-cross the fence.

On Grey Knotts

We can see our way ahead clearly now - the mostly level, grassy plateau that fills the space between **Grey Knotts** and **Brandreth** stretches out before us. Beyond, we can see a clear path climbing **Green Gable** and, just to its right, is the impressive, rocky face of **Gable Crag**.

Heading away from the fence we've just crossed, we stride out across the grass, heading straight towards **Great Gable** (SSW). There is a faint path on the ground, but it has an annoying tendency to disappear at times.

Having walked about 250 yards from Wp.4, we see a fence a little way to our right. For ease of navigation, and to enjoy our first superb views of **Ennerdale Water** and **Crummock Water**, we head for this fence and follow it (SW). When it kinks right, we leave it and keep straight ahead, aiming for the rusty fencepost on the hilltop just above us.

(Last time I was up here, there were piles of new wooden fenceposts scattered about these fells, so it is likely that there will be new fences in place by the time you read this. Bear this in mind when using the fences for navigation.)

From the stony, desolate top of **Brandreth** (Wp.5 75M), we follow the line of rusty fenceposts straight down the fell (S) until we hit a clear, cairned path coming in from the right (Wp.6 81M). Turning left, we pass a series of small but pretty tarns on our right and then begin the climb on to **Green Gable**.

It's not too steep an ascent, but the annoyingly stony path prevents us from really striding out and enjoying the stroll. The pleasing symmetry of **Ennerdale's** slopes draws our eyes away to the west, where tall, upright **Pillar** looms sentinel-like over what remains of the valley's dark plantations.

But it is to **Great Gable** that we look when we reach the top of **Green Gable** (Wp.7 111M). Its monstrous north face is turned towards us - a huge mass of sheer grey rock and scree fans.

We plunge down the south ridge of **Green Gable** to **Windy Gap** (Wp.8 118M) for a short breather before the final, steep pull on to **Great Gable** itself. At first, we are on a narrow path that edges around the south-eastern side of **Gable Crag**, but then we veer right and are faced with a steep incline criss-crossed by loose rock and gritty paths. It's hard to decide which way to go. Those who fancy a rocky scramble should head to the left of this tangled mess; those who prefer not to have to use their hands should keep right.

Either way, there are difficulties. The loose path weaving its way up to the right is extremely unstable in places; if you're using rock to pull yourself up, be careful because much of it is unstable and will easily come away from the bedrock. Once this section has been conquered, all that remains between us and the summit is a jumble of smooth stones, not unlike the large pebbles you find on some beaches, and you know how difficult they are to walk on!

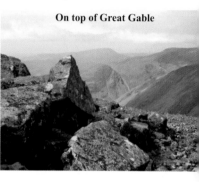
On top of Great Gable

Finally, we reach the summit of **Great Gable** (Wp.9 146M), our efforts rewarded by fantastic views in all directions and a wonderful sense of satisfaction. It's as if you're on top of the world! The **Scafell** range seems to be just a stone's throw away, with the great, dark gash of **Piers Gill** clearly visible from this angle. Making their first appearances are **Windermere**, far to the south-east, and **Wastwater** (SW).

The memorial on Great Gable

The two smaller bodies of water just below us to the south-east are **Styhead Tarn** and **Sprinkling Tarn**, the higher of the two.

Just after the First World War, the Fell and Rock Climbing Club purchased much of **Great Gable** as a memorial to members who had died during the conflict. A plaque, bearing a relief map of the area and the names of the fallen, can be found on the north side of the summit rocks. Every year, walkers and climbers make a pilgrimage to the summit on Remembrance Sunday for the commemorative service that has been held on the mountain ever since.

You'll want some time to rest at the top, to soak up the surroundings, to wander to every corner of the summit and see the views from every possible angle, but when it is finally time to leave we must retrace our steps as far as

Windy Gap. In the mist, it is easy to get lost up here and end up following the wrong line of cairns down the mountain. We need to head NE at first to pick up a line down through the difficult, steep section.

Ennerdale from Windy Gap

Turning left at **Windy Gap** (Wp.8 178M), we carefully inch our way down what has become little more than a scree shute. To our left, climbers are making their laborious way up **Gable Crag**. Turning right at a T-junction at the bottom (Wp.10 197M), we stride out along a mostly level path with sweeping views down **Ennerdale**.

This is **Moses' Trod**, a packhorse route, once used to transport slate from **Honister** to **Wasdale**. It was named after a quarryman who, legend has it, illegally made whisky and then smuggled it across the fells to **Wasdale** with his pony-loads of slate. The remains of a hut high on **Gable Crag** have been linked to Moses and suggested as a site of one of his stills. It is located in an exposed position midway up the buttress to the left of **Central Gully**. The site is known by climbers as **Smugglers' Retreat**.

Gone now are the rocky slopes of the Gables as we wander leisurely along this lovely path, surrounded by Herdwicks grazing on the luscious grass. As we approach a fence cutting straight across our path, we bear right at a fork (Wp.11 219M) and cross the fence via a stile. The path is unclear here, but, 50 yards beyond the stile, we bear left along a distinct, cairned route (Wp.12 221M). **Buttermere** and **Crummock Water** reappear to our left.

Nearing the messy slate workings on **Fleetwith**, we reach a wide, raised path (Wp.13 247M). This is the track of an old tramway that was used to move slate down to **Honister Pass**. We join it at its highest point, named on OS maps as **Drum House**. This building, of which only the foundations remain, housed the tram's winding gear. Turning right, we head downhill. On reaching a vehicle track at the bottom of the incline (Wp.14 266M), we turn right and follow it round as it passes in front of the **Honister Slate Mine** shop and visitor centre, where you can buy refreshments (or go on a mine tour if you've got time). Passing an open-fronted shed on our left, we go through a pedestrian gate (Wp.1) to re-enter the car park.

You can see practically all of the Lake District's major fell groupings from the top of **Glaramara** (782 metres) - it's a wonderful place to stand on a clear day. **Allen Crags** (785 metres) is even better; a stone's throw from **Bow Fell, Great End** and **Scafell Pike**, it's dwarfed by its imposing neighbours.

There's only one significant difficulty on this walk - the short rock climb that faces us as we reach the base of the **Glaramara** buttress - but this can be easily avoided.

4/5   4¾ H   8.8 miles/14.2km   871m   871m   2

Access by car: The walk starts from the farm at **Seathwaite** in **Borrowdale** (GR NY235121). From **Keswick**, follow the B5289 **Borrowdale** road for about 7.5 miles and then, on the edge of **Seatoller**, turn left along a narrow lane. The lane ends at the farm and there is plenty of parking along the roadside. Be careful not to block any field entrances or the turning circle.

Access by bus: Seathwaite is not served by public transport, but nearby **Seatoller** is served all year by bus N°79, the Borrowdale Rambler, from **Keswick**. In the summer, the N°77/77A (Honister Rambler) also passes through **Seatoller** on its circular route between **Keswick** and **Buttermere** (see appendix).

Seathwaite

Passing in front of the farmhouse (Wp.1 0M), we turn left at the footpath sign towards **Thorneythwaite** and then go through a gate to enter a field. Keeping close to the wall on our left, we go through another gate and, for the next 25 minutes, cross rough grazing land at the base of some steep slopes to our right. During the summer this valley path is a delight, brought to life by the sound of birdsong and lambs bleating; come the wet weather, however, it can become a muddy mess.

Reaching a gap in a wall with old wooden gate posts on either side (Wp.2 26M), we obey the yellow waymarkers that indicate we leave the vehicle-wide track here by turning right to walk with a wall on our left. We then turn right at a surfaced lane (Wp.3 28M).

Going through a gate on our right at a public footpath sign beside a wooden stile (Wp.4 32M), we begin to climb gently on a wide, stony track. Slowly gaining height, the slightly muffled sound of **Combe Gill** comes to us from over the wall to our left. We catch our first glimpse of it, cascading down the channel's bare rock, after passing through a gate that gives us access to the open fell (51M).

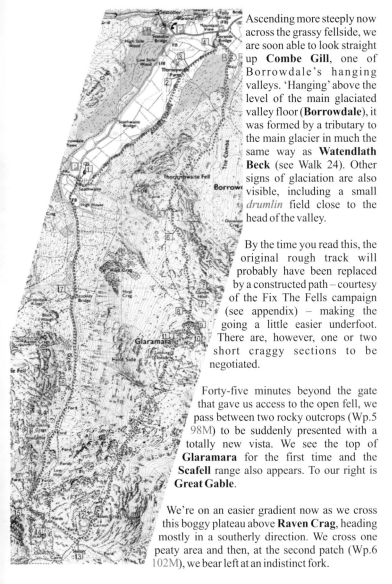

Ascending more steeply now across the grassy fellside, we are soon able to look straight up **Combe Gill**, one of Borrowdale's hanging valleys. 'Hanging' above the level of the main glaciated valley floor (**Borrowdale**), it was formed by a tributary to the main glacier in much the same way as **Watendlath Beck** (see Walk 24). Other signs of glaciation are also visible, including a small *drumlin* field close to the head of the valley.

By the time you read this, the original rough track will probably have been replaced by a constructed path – courtesy of the Fix The Fells campaign (see appendix) – making the going a little easier underfoot. There are, however, one or two short craggy sections to be negotiated.

Forty-five minutes beyond the gate that gave us access to the open fell, we pass between two rocky outcrops (Wp.5 98M) to be suddenly presented with a totally new vista. We see the top of **Glaramara** for the first time and the **Scafell** range also appears. To our right is **Great Gable**.

We're on an easier gradient now as we cross this boggy plateau above **Raven Crag**, heading mostly in a southerly direction. We cross one peaty area and then, at the second patch (Wp.6 102M), we bear left at an indistinct fork.

Both paths end up in the same place, but our chosen route follows higher ground while the one to the right tends to be soggier. Keep to the main path at all times now. As it bends a sharp right a little after climbing through a stony gully, keep the faith and don't be tempted by the faint path that continues straight ahead (Wp.7 119M). The same is true four minutes later when the path again turns sharp right to cross an often water-logged area via stepping stones (Wp.8 123M). The cairn-topped summit to the left is <u>not</u> **Glaramara**; we are heading for that steep buttress just on the other side of the next uphill section.

As we reach the base of the buttress (Wp.9 130M), the way ahead may not seem obvious at first. The conventional route goes straight up the steep rockface. Walking poles need to be stashed away safely, because you'll need your hands. Safe ledges, where we can rest and decide on our next moves, divide the 7-metre climb into easily manageable sections. The worst is over within the first few manoeuvres, but if you can't face the climb (or the rock is icy), there is an easier alternative. Simply turn right at Wp.9 and follow the base of the buttress until you come to a grassy area. Turn left here and ascend the slope until you reach a cairned route heading steeply up the rockface to the left.

Looking across to the Gables from Glaramara

This eventually leads to the summit cairn (Wp.10 142M) and its magnificent 360-degree views. (For those climbing the front of the buttress, the summit cairn is the one to the right of the route.) Most of the major fell groupings are visible from here, including the **Langdales** and the **Coniston** fells.

Having rested for a while in the cosy little shelter tucked away on the north side of the summit cairn, we need to find the path that will take us in a generally south-westerly direction across the wide, rocky ridge to **Allen Crags**. At the southern end of the rocks housing the summit cairn and shelter, we turn right to cross sometimes boggy and sometimes rocky pathless terrain. There is a faint track heading on to the craggy cairn-topped knoll ahead and to our right, but we can avoid this unnecessary climb by passing to the left of the knoll. (Pedantic peak-baggers may want to head on to this knoll as it is fractionally higher than the cairn we visited at Wp.10, although Wp.10 is generally regarded as the top of **Glaramara**.)

We soon see a path coming down from the knoll via a grassy rake and we join this path as it starts to head downhill over some boulders (Wp.11 148M).

To say the way ahead is undulating is something of an understatement. First, we head down; then we go up; then, with the magnificent north face of **Great End** straight ahead, we descend; then it's up again…And so it goes, all the way to **Allen Crags**, across very rocky terrain. It's easy to lose the route among the rocks, so keep your eyes peeled for cairns guiding the way. At first we head WSW, veering more to the SW after about half a mile.

The Langdales from the ridge path

The top of **Allen Crags** (Wp.12 207M) is marked by a mere cairn, but I often feel this wonderful location needs something more to single it out. From here, we can look straight across the pass at **Esk Hause** to the **Irish Sea**. **Esk Pike** and **Bow Fell** (SSE) are a stone's throw away, **Great End** still dominates the view to the west and, heading west from the pass, is a path leading to **Scafell**

Great Gable from Allen Crags

Pike - it looks tempting from here, but it would add three miles and almost 400 metres of ascent to an already hard day.

Shooting down from **Allen Crags** on a steep, loose path (SSW), we turn right at a junction marked by a large cairn (Wp.13 212M). Having forded two streams, we join up with a track coming in from the left (Wp.14 216M) and then, 260 yards after this junction, leave the track by turning right to cross the steep-sided gully below us (Wp.15 219M).

Above Ruddy Gill

Skirting the top of **Ruddy Gill**, a rocky gorge with a few small trees clinging miraculously to its sheer walls, we begin the long, tiresome descent on a constructed path.

The many interesting gullies, waterfalls and pools help relieve the tedium of the relentless downhill slog. We cross one bridge (Wp.16 248M) and then walk with **Grains Gill** on our right.

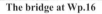

The bridge at Wp.16

Turning right at a T-junction (Wp.17 265M), we cross the gill via the humpback **Stockley Bridge** and then veer left to follow the clear track back to the farm at **Seathwaite** (Wp.1 285M).

Stockley Bridge

There's a small tearoom at the farm which serves drinks and homemade cakes. Alternatively, **Seatoller**, just over a mile away, is home to **The Yew Tree Country Restaurant**.

Sale Fell (359 metres) is a lovely little grassy top close to the northern edge of the Lake District. Although popular with local people, you'll rarely see it mentioned in guidebooks to the area.

On this walk, we explore the fell's high ground and get some wonderful views of nearby **Skiddaw**. There is a short but easy ascent to the summit and the paths are all clear on the ground. Save this one for a clear summer's evening when you can watch the sun setting over the west coast.

2 | 1H 20M | 2.8 miles/4.5km | 258m / 258m | 3

Access by car: You'll have to drive to the start of the walk as there is no bus route. The walk starts from a roadside parking area 200 yards north-east of **St Margaret's Church**, near **Wythop Mill**, GR NY191302. To reach the parking area from **Keswick**, drive north-west along the A66 (towards **Cockermouth**) for 7.3 miles until you reach the turn for **Wythop Mill** and the **Pheasant Inn**. (Ignore the first turning for the **Pheasant Inn**.) Turn left here, take the first road on the right and then turn right again when you reach the pub. The parking area is two-thirds of a mile up this road on the right.

Alternatively, if coming from **Cockermouth**, you turn right at the **Wythop Mill/Pheasant Inn** exit 5.4 miles after joining the A66. **The Pheasant**, incidentally, serves good quality pub food if you fancy a bite to eat at the end of the walk.

From the parking area (Wp.1 0M), we cross the road to go through the gate towards **Kelswick** and up the track. Soon after passing a bench and going through a gap in a drystone wall, we swing to the right as a path joins us from the left (Wp.2 6M). As the wide path starts swinging to the SW, we see **Ling Fell** (373 metres) ahead of us. We soon encounter a drystone wall to our right and then turn left along a grassy path heading straight up the

Heading onto Sale Fell

On Sale Fell

open fellside (Wp.3 18M). In 66 yards, we bear right at a fork to ascend the southern edge of the fell (Wp.4 19M).

Ignoring a faint path off to the right, we continue uphill, soon catching our first sighting of **Skiddaw** to the east. As the sun starts going down, the Lake District's fourth highest

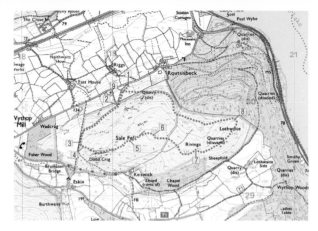

Cyclist at sunset on Sale Fell

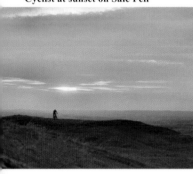

mountain may even take on a glorious pink tinge - stunning all who witness the sight into silence. The view to the NW is opening out too, with the perfect bump of **Criffel** standing out clearly as we look across the **Solway** to the coast of **Dumfries & Galloway**. It's hardly surprising that we have to share **Sale Fell** with dog walkers, runners and a few cyclists, all out to enjoy the last of the day's sunshine.

Sale Fell Summit

We soon cross to the northern side of the fell where we join up with a path coming in from the left and, in another 55 yards, we bear left at a fork (Wp.5 32M). Seven more minutes of easy ascent and we reach the cairn-topped summit of this delightful little fell (Wp.6 39M). It's a wonderful place to linger.

Skiddaw, from the summit of Sale Fell

Eventually dragging ourselves away from the top, we shoot down from the summit cairn (ESE) to pass through a gate in a wall. Ignoring the faint path off to the left, we stroll along the wide track to a gap in what is left of a tumbledown wall.

Again ignoring a path off to the left, we aim for the large cairn on the hillside ahead of us (SE). Beyond the cairn we swing left (E) and soon meet up with another path coming in from the left (Wp.7 47M).

Ignoring a path off to the right, we quickly climb on to a short but delightful grassy ridge with the massive bulk of **Skiddaw** dominating the view ahead. **Bassenthwaite Lake** becomes visible as we reach the highest point of the ridge, as does **Keswick** to the SE.

On reaching the wall at the edge of **Wythop Woods** (Wp.8 58M), we turn left to head downhill. The dense forest to our left is home to the Lake District's only pair of osprey. These fish-eating birds of prey returned to Cumbria in 2001 after a 150-year absence and now look set to stay; they spend the summer in the county, flying to their nest in April and returning to Africa in September. If you want to catch a glimpse of these powerful creatures and their chicks, high-powered telescopes have been set up on a viewing platform in **Dodd Wood** on the east side of **Bassenthwaite Lake**. There's also a giant video wall showing live footage from the nest at the Forestry Commission's **Whinlatter Visitor Centre**.

Having forded a small stream (67M), we go through a gate to continue our downward trend on a pleasant grassy track. As the ground to our right drops away, the northern end of **Bassenthwaite Lake** is revealed. We cross a tumbledown section of a drystone wall (75M) and follow the track as it bears left towards **St Margaret's**. This church was built in 1865 to replace the old **Wythop Church**, the ruins of which can still be seen on the southern side of **Sale Fell** near **Kelswick**. The old church was built during the reign of Queen Mary (1553-58) and an open-air service is still held on its former site every August.

On reaching a junction near the bench that we passed at the beginning of the walk (Wp.9 79M) we turn right and continue down to the gate where we started (Wp.1 80M).

Most people who head up on to **Causey Pike** (672 metres) or **Barrow** (455 metres) invariably do so en route to the higher mountains of the spectacular **Coledale** Round (see Walk 31). But if we spend any time on these two "lesser" fells, we'll soon discover that they are more than mere stepping stones to higher and greater things; combined, they provide an interesting and varied day's walking along two delightful ridges.

This walk can also be used as an alternative start to the **Coledale** Round (walk 31). We simply leave the **Causey Pike** route at Wp.11, the saddle between **Causey Pike** and **Sail**. This corresponds with Wp.6 on walk 31.

Access by car: parking area (GR NY 232217) on the **Newlands Valley** road 1.3 miles south of **Braithwaite**.

Stonycroft Gill

From the parking area (Wp.1 0M), we cross the road and head left along the wide, gorse-edged track that runs parallel with the road for a while. As the track bends to the right, away from the road, we climb easily on gravel. After almost half a mile (750 yards), just before the gradient steepens a little, we take the path off to the left (Wp.2 15M), running parallel with the main track for a short while and then dropping down to **Stonycroft Gill**. At the lowest point in the path, we ford the stream (Wp.3 19M), resisting the urge to rest a while in this pretty, secluded spot - it looks like a good spot for a picnic, but it's still too early in the day for thoughts of lunch!

Having dunked our boots in the stream, we stroll along the mostly level path as it heads left. Yes, we are coming back on ourselves - it may seem like a convoluted route at first, but the alternative is to head straight up the busier path on **Rowling End** and miss out on this lovely valley and a peaceful start to the day. And heading straight on to the ridge, we'd miss the surprise view at **Sleet Hause**, but more about that later…

Reaching a junction with another track, we turn right (Wp.4 28M) and start to climb steadily. **Causey Pike** is the knobbly top ahead and slightly to the left; in the distance, we can see **Grisedale Pike** (791 metres); and, on our right are the slopes of **Barrow**, still recovering from a three-day-long fell fire thought to have been started by a cigarette being carelessly discarded during tinder-dry conditions in April 2003.

The walk up these heather and bilberry-clad slopes is gentle at first, but we're being lulled into a false sense of security…

Abruptly, the path bears left (Wp.5 50M) and we're having to battle our way up a loose, rocky incline. It's a tedious quarter-mile, but we're rewarded at **Sleet Hause** (Wp.6 68M) when we're suddenly confronted by a magnificent vista of mountains. Straight ahead are the fells of the **Robinson** Round; in the distance, to the right (SW) is **High Stile**; and the **Helvellyn** range is to the far left (SE).

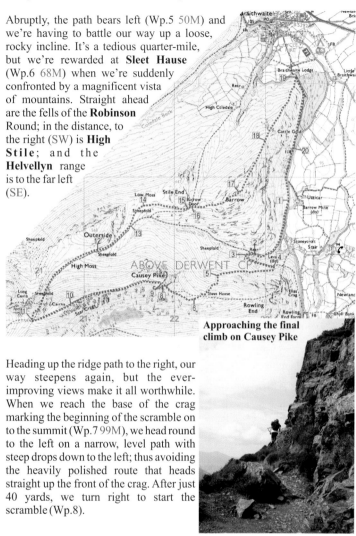

Approaching the final climb on Causey Pike

Heading up the ridge path to the right, our way steepens again, but the ever-improving views make it all worthwhile. When we reach the base of the crag marking the beginning of the scramble on to the summit (Wp.7 99M), we head round to the left on a narrow, level path with steep drops down to the left; thus avoiding the heavily polished route that heads straight up the front of the crag. After just 40 yards, we turn right to start the scramble (Wp.8).

It's a short clamber and we soon reach the lower, but not lesser, of **Causey Pike**'s two summits (Wp.9 110M), from where we can just about make out **Scafell Pike** to the south.

The ridge path stretches away from us invitingly - narrow, but not narrow enough to induce vertigo. We stride out, heading downhill at first and then slightly uphill to the fell's true summit (Wp.10 126M). There is a sense of having been cheated - how can this cairn, so easy to reach along the ridge, be 35 metres higher than the eastern summit, which you arrive at puffing and sweating?

From the summit, we drop quickly down to the saddle between **Causey Pike** and **Sail** (Wp.11 134M), where we turn right. We need to be careful as we descend this steep, narrow path because the surface can be loose in places.

Grisedale Pike seen from across the valley

It's easy to be distracted by the views across the valley to the incredibly long and steep south-east face of **Grisedale Pike**, but we'll have plenty of opportunity to look up from the path when the slippery section is behind us. And it soon is behind us –the going getting a lot better as the gradient eases.

As we descend, we ignore any paths off to the left, always sticking to the main track until we have passed a tumbledown old sheepfold below us to the right (Wp.12 162M).

Beyond here, we need to watch out for our path off - it is the second on the left, 500 yards after the sheepfold (Wp.13). Another path soon joins us from the left as we amble along and, when the path forks, we bear right (Wp.14 171M). This pleasant path contours the side of the fell until we join up with a clearer route coming in from the right (Wp.15 176M). We don't stay with this path for long though - 20 yards after joining it, we reach a fork where we bear right on to a grassier path (Wp.16). This quickly swings round to climb the obvious ridge path on to **Barrow**.

After the climb up on to **Causey Pike**, the way on to **Barrow** is a doddle and it's all over in a flash - before we know it, we stumble upon the summit (Wp.17 195M) and its impressive, uninterrupted view of **Skiddaw**. Then, heading down the lovely path on the fell's north-eastern ridge, we have good views of **D e r w e n t w a t e r** and **Bassenthwaite Lake**.

Braithwaite Lodge farm

Half way down the fell, we bear right at a fork (Wp.18 208M). When we reach a small footpath sign at the base of the fell (Wp.19 223M), we turn right towards **Newlands** along a level path with woodland to our left. This path then drops gently down bracken and gorse-covered slopes to the road (Wp.20 229M) where we turn right. The parking area (Wp.1) is just a few minutes' stroll ahead on the left.

29 BUTTERMERE TO HONISTER via ROBINSON & DALE HEAD

A relentless climb on grassy slopes, a soggy plod across **Buttermere Moss** and then another steep section. As a beginning to a walk description, it doesn't hold much promise, but I can almost guarantee that you'll barely notice any discomfort from tired calf muscles or damp boots when you're surrounded by such magnificent mountain scenery. And then, once you're on that ridge - airy, but not frighteningly so - all your worldly troubles will disappear.

This linear walk takes us on to **Robinson** (737 metres) and **Dale Head** (753 metres) from **Buttermere** and then descends to **Honister Pass** where we catch the N°77/77A Honister Rambler bus back to **Buttermere**. Unless you are able to arrange alternative transport, this walk is only possible in the summer because the Honister Rambler doesn't run in the winter months.

Access by car: The walk starts from the Lake District National Park car park at **Buttermere** on the B5289, about 13 miles south-west of **Keswick** or 10 miles south-east of **Cockermouth**.

Access by bus: **Buttermere** is served by the N°77/77A Honister Rambler circular bus route from Easter until the end of October and the N°263 Ennerdale Rambler (see appendix).

Leaving the car park at **Buttermere** (Wp.1 0M), we keep the **Bridge Inn** on our left and then turn right along the road (Wp.2 2M). Just after passing the tiny village church on some high ground to our left, we turn left at the road junction (Wp.3 4M). And so we begin our short, sharp climb on to **Robinson** - on asphalt. Almost exactly 300 yards after the junction at Wp.3, we say goodbye to the road as we turn right at a wooden footpath sign (Wp.4 10M), which indicates that the top of **Robinson** is now just one mile away. Only one mile? How hard can it be?

The first 45 minutes of climbing are relentless, but it's a fantastic path – quiet and with constantly changing views as it charts a winding course up the steep, grassy fellside. This is the Moss Road, an old route that was once used to bring peat down from **Buttermere Moss**. We're on a wide green swathe cutting through the bracken at first, but the route soon gets narrower and, in places, rockier as we gain height. As we approach the top, we have to clamber around the head of a gully (Wp5 46M). The rocks get very slippery here in damp conditions, so watch your footing!

Suddenly, the ascent stops (Wp.6 55M) and we stand on **High Snockrigg** looking across **Buttermere Moss** to **Robinson**. This large area of marshland, sitting so high up on the fells, comes as something of a surprise. It's about half a mile across north to south and slightly more west to east. It looks quite daunting when you first see it on the map, but as long as you stick to the clear path, your boots should stay reasonably dry. We follow the path to our right as it heads slightly downhill with magnificent views of **Great Gable** and **Hay Stacks** straight ahead of us. As we veer left to cross **Buttermere Moss**, the fells to our left belong to the **Coledale** Horseshoe with **Knott Rigg** forming the attractive, low-level ridge in the middle ground.

Mineral-veined rocks

Approaching the base of **Robinson**, we can see our path cutting a faint north-easterly line up the steep fellside. Like all the paths I have used so far today, this one isn't particularly well-walked, but it's easy to follow when you're on it. It is steep and, in places, loose, but there is no scrambling involved - the tricky sections look worse from below than they actually are. The last section of the climb is a delight for geology enthusiasts as it passes through an area of multi-coloured boulders, each with a variety of different mineral veins passing through it.

As we reach the top of **Robinson** (Wp.7 97M), marked by a cairn on top of a small rocky outcrop, we are presented with a magnificent panorama of mountains - all four of the Lake District's 3000-foot fells are visible from here, although **Great Gable** blocks the view of the actual summit of **Scafell Pike**. (The more observant, by the way, will have realised by now that the signpost at Wp.4 is way off the mark with its 'one-mile-to-Robinson' claim!). Heading south from the summit, we follow the well-walked track down to a fence where we bear left to descend more steeply. Ignoring a path off to the left at the bottom of this drop (Wp.8 115M), we begin climbing again. We still have a fence to our right at first, but this soon becomes just a line of rusty fence posts.

On the ridge

As we stride out along the superb ridge, the incredibly craggy and scree-ridden fell to our right is **Fleetwith**; over its western ridge, we get a clear view of **Hay Stacks**; and beyond that is **Pillar** - layer upon wonderful layer of mountains. Having picked our way easily through some rocky bands as **Hindscarth Edge** narrows, we reach the huge cairn at the top of **Dale Head**, the highest point on today's walk (Wp.9 157M). I could wax lyrical about this wonderful spot, but I think

I'll save it for another day - walk 30, in fact!

From the summit, we turn right, following a line of cairns down the fellside. The first cairn has been built up around a rusty fence post. This path will eventually lead us all the way down to **Honister Pass**. It's a relatively easy descent, keeping the fence on our right for most of the way. We pass an old quarry on the other side of the fence, but the workings on **Dale Head** are disused now. It's another story on **Fleetwith**, however. We can clearly see the many gaping gashes that rip into the mountainside, giving generations of miners access to the green slate that has made **Honister** famous.

Looking down from Hindscarth Edge

Some of these wounds are part of disused workings now, but there is no doubt that **Honister Slate Mine** is still a busy place.

As we rapidly lose height, the noise drifts up to remind us that the Lake District is not just a playground for people who love the great outdoors; it is a place where people live and work - the rumble of mines trucks as they make their way up the fellside, the hum of the generators and the distinctive tinny, ringing clatter of slate on slate as visitors fill their car boots for a tenner.

Nearing **Honister Pass**, we cross a stile in the fence to our right (Wp.10 192M) and then continue downhill to reach the B5289 at the pass (Wp.11 195M). The building across the road to our left is the youth hostel, and the bus back to **Buttermere** stops at the entrance to its car park. If you've got time before the next bus, a visit to the **Honister Slate Mine** for a tour of the workings is highly recommended.

If you haven't got time to enjoy a tour, the visitor centre - just along the road to our right - serves refreshments. Alternatively, there are two pubs, a café and a wonderful ice-cream shop when you get back to **Buttermere**.

You can't beat a good horseshoe walk when you really want to get out and stretch your legs, and this particular horseshoe takes a lot of beating. We follow the traditional way on to this round - via **Cat Bells** (451 metres) – and then continue the ascent via **Maiden Moor** (576 metres), **High Spy** (653 metres) and up to **Dale Head** (753 metres) and its magnificent views, before a ridge walk along **Hindscarth Edge**. The descent from the final top, **Hindscarth** (727 metres), is gorgeous - you'll be willing it to never end.

There are several escape routes on the way up to **Dale Head**. You can turn left or right at the pass between **Cat Bells** and **Maiden Moor** and then follow the fellside paths that head north, back towards the car park. From Wp.8, instead of crossing the beck, you can follow it downstream all the way to **Little Town**. From Wp.9, instead of bearing left on to **Dale Head**, there is a path to the right of the cairn that will take you down the valley to **Little Town**. Finally, if you encounter difficulties once on the top of **Dale Head**, there is a path from the summit heading down the fell in a southerly direction to **Honister Pass**, just over a mile below.

Access by car: The walk starts from the small parking area near **Skelgill** (GR NY245211). From **Keswick**, pick up the A66 heading towards **Cockermouth** and then take the left turn for **Portinscale**. Follow this road for 2.1 miles until you reach a series of climbing bends. As you leave the woody area, turn right on the sharp left-hand bend and the parking area is just ahead on your left. The start of the walk is not served by buses, but it is possible to get the Keswick Launch across **Derwentwater** to **Hawes End** and then walk the 0.35 miles up to the car park (see appendix).

Wasting no time with a gentle walk in, we begin the climb straight from the car park (Wp.1 0M), taking the path that heads up through the bracken at the eastern end of the parking area. As we catch our first glimpse of **Derwentwater** glinting in the morning light, we bear right to continue uphill (Wp.2 4M). It's a slow slog on to **Cat Bells** and there's a false alarm along the way. As we reach the first craggy section - with its memorial to Thomas Arthur Leonard, founder of the 'open-air movement in this country' - it's best to head to the left to avoid scrambling on polished, slippery rock.

The path onto Cat Bells

Soon after, we reach a false top, which might fool you into thinking that it's the summit of **Cat Bells**. No, the true summit is another steep climb away. There's a bit of scrambling involved on the way up, but it's fairly easy.

The top of **Cat Bells** (Wp.3 50M) is normally heaving

with walkers, but if you've started early, you could have it to yourself. Far below is **Brackenburn**, the former home of New Zealand-born writer Sir Hugh Walpole. He lived in Cumbria from 1924 until his death in 1941, calling **Brackenburn** his "little paradise on Cat Bells". Originally a bungalow built of Honister slate in 1909, he enlarged it and converted the upper story of the nearby garage into a study which eventually housed his library of 30,000 books and his collection of paintings. Literary visitors to the house included JB Priestly, Arthur Ransome and WH Auden.

Shooting down from the summit, we reach the *hause* between **Cat Bells** and **Maiden Moor** as we draw level with the southern end of **Derwentwater**. Our climb up on to **Maiden Moor** from here is not as steep as the route on to **Cat Bells**, but it can seem a bit of a plod after our earlier exertions.

As the path levels off slightly and we get our first decent views south (Wp.4 84M), we turn right along what I call the aficionado's path. You wouldn't know it was there; it's partly hidden by the rocky outcrop beside the path.

M o s t walkers keep sheep-like to the main path t h a t c u t s uninspiringly across the dull moorland top, but our route heads over to the western edge for some superb views. The Coledale Round is off to our right, but closer in are **R o b i n s o n** and **Hindscarth**, both with tempting ridge paths plunging from their northern ends. As we reach the highest point on this path (Wp.5 97M) marked by a small cairn to the left of our route - we can see straight ahead to the craggy northern face of **Dale Head** and, just appearing in the gap between **Dale Head** and **High Spy**, are **Great Gable** and the **Scafell** group. Six more minutes and we rejoin the main path (Wp.6 103M) to start the relatively easy ascent of **High Spy**. This is a kind horseshoe! The third climb of the day and it's by far the easiest! Are we being lulled into a false sense of security?

High Spy summit

Ignoring a faint path off to the left on the way up, we stick to the wide, cairned route all the way to the huge cairn that marks the summit (Wp.7 130M). The view south opens out dramatically now - straight ahead of us are the Lake District's most magnificent peaks, including **Bow Fell, Great End, Scafell Pike, Scafell** and **Great Gable**.

We lose quite a bit of height over the next two-thirds of a mile. You see that small tarn below us and slightly to the right? Well, that's our next destination – **Dalehead Tarn**.

Dalehead Tarn

The path down is rocky in places, but it shouldn't present us with any difficulties. After fording a beck that also forms the tarn's outlet stream (Wp.8 150M), we clamber up to the water's edge and keep it on our left as we head to the path on to **Dale Head**. (Note that the path no longer goes around the southern end of the tarn as shown on OS maps.)

Looking north from Dale Head

You remember that kind horseshoe that we talked about earlier? Well, it ends here - the route on to **Dale Head** is steep. First, we're on loose stone, but then we find our way on to a constructed path. Slowly, we head upwards. At the top of the constructed path (Wp.9 172M), we get a great view down the U-shaped dale with **Skiddaw** perfectly framed at the end. But, oh what a cruel horseshoe! If you thought the climb was over, you're mistaken. We now have to bear left for the final pull on to **Dale Head** proper, zigzagging our way up to the summit cairn (Wp.10 187M). But what a fantastic top it is when we get there! There's that great view down the valley, of course, but it's to the south and south-west that the eyes are drawn. The **Scafell** group and **Great Gable** are just a stone's throw away it seems. Then there's **Kirk Fell**, magnificent **Pillar** and the **High Stile** range. On a clear day, you can just about make out the **Mull of Galloway**, and the **Isle of Man** is visible in the gap between **Pillar** and **High Stile**.

Striding out along the delightful ridge path (WNW), we have the beautiful blue waters of **Buttermere** far below us. Dropping into a slight dip on the ridge, we turn right along a narrower path (Wp.11 204M). **Hindscarth** is our last top of the day and there's an easy stroll ahead of us to get to the summit. Turning right (N) at the next path junction (Wp.12 210M), the summit shelter (Wp.13) is just a six-minute walk ahead. From here, we drop down (NNE) to another, larger shelter, from where the descent proper begins. The ground underfoot is loose, but walkers' boots have carved out a zigzagging route that makes the going easier. Fifteen minutes beyond the larger shelter, the gradient eases and we amble along a pleasant, grassy ridge. As we make our way along a narrow path on the eastern edge of the fell, we encounter heathery slopes that form a beautiful carpet of purple in the late summer. That dark ridge to our right belongs to **Maiden Moor** and **High Spy**, the first half of our horseshoe today.

As the ridge narrows, our way down steepens and we have a few rocky sections to negotiate - nothing too tricky though. Reaching a fence/wall (291M), we keep to the path as it bears right and passes beneath some spoil heaps. This area was home to one of Cumberland's most important mines in the 16th century - the **Goldscope Mine**. It was opened by German engineers working for The Company of Mines Royal in 1565. Copper and lead were mined here, as well as smaller quantities of silver and gold. The mine was originally called 'Gotes Gab' (German for God's gift), but this deteriorated over time to Goldscope.

Newlands Church

Reaching the farm track (Wp.14 297M), we turn left to enter the farmyard. This is not a right of way - it is a permitted path only, so it is possible for the farmer to close it from time to time. In the summer, **Low Snab Farm** serves up pots of tea and slices of cake - welcome refreshment after so long on the ridge. And, when we reach the other end of the farm track (Wp.15 305M), we may be lucky enough to find **Newlands Church** open and serving drinks.

Turning right at the church, we soon reach the road (Wp.16 308M), where we turn right again. The next set of cottages form part of **Little Town**. Beatrix Potter was a frequent visitor to this area and it figures highly in 'The Tale of Mrs Tiggy-Winkle'. The character, Lucie of Little Town, was based on the daughter of the vicar of **Newlands Church**. After passing the cottages, we turn right along a rough lane (Wp.17 318M) towards **Skelgill**. A series of gates, bridges and stiles guides us across several fields and down on to a lane at **Skelgill** (Wp.18 339M). Turning right, it's a straightforward stroll back along the lane to the parking area from which we started the walk.

I know I said that the **Newlands** Round takes a lot of beating, but … well, here it is … the horseshoe to beat the **Newlands** Round. In fact, in my humble opinion, it's the horseshoe to beat all horseshoes in the northern Lakes.

The **Coledale** Round described here takes in **Sail** (773 metres), **Crag Hill** (839 metres), **Hopegill Head** (770 metres) and **Grisedale Pike** (791 metres), but it can be tailored to suit the walkers' needs. There are a number of ways to shorten it and part of Walk 28 (**Causey Pike** and **Barrow**) can be added on at the beginning to make it longer. You'll be tired by the end of the walk, but a sense of achievement will keep that smile on your face for a day or two afterwards.

The one obvious escape route is at **Coledale Hause**, about half way through the round, where you can turn right to return alongside **Coledale Beck**.

Access by car: The **Coledale** Round starts in the village of **Braithwaite**, just off the A66, two miles west of **Keswick**. If you're driving from **Keswick**, head through the village, passing the Royal Oak pub on your left and then take the second left, signposted Youth Centre and **Coledale**. Turn right immediately after the tiny, white-washed Methodist church and there is room for about a dozen cars in the parking bays on the right (GR NY229236).

Access by bus: Braithwaite is served all year by bus X5, **Penrith** to **Workington** via **Keswick** and **Cockermouth**. In the summer, the 77/77A (Honister Rambler) passes through the village on its circular route between **Keswick** and **Buttermere** (see appendix).

Standing with the pretty church on our left (Wp.1 0M), we cross the asphalt lane and walk straight up the track opposite, coming out at **The Coledale Inn** (1M). The famous Cumberland Pencil Company, established in 1868, was originally located in **Braithwaite**; this building, now a pub, was the factory manager's home. The company only moved to **Keswick** at the end of the nineteenth century when the **Braithwaite** factory was destroyed by fire.

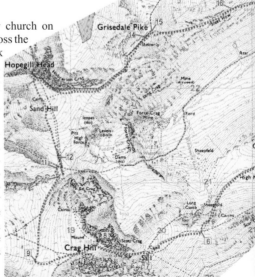

Turning left along the quiet road, we climb very gradually with several nicely situated cottages and bungalows on our right. Going through a gate (Wp.2 6M), we amble up the rough track beyond, accompanied by the soothing sound of the beck below, welcoming us on to the open fells and finally drowning out any noise from the busy A66.

Heading up to Barrow Door

As the track turns sharp right towards a gate and a ruined building (Wp.3 15M), we leave it by keeping straight ahead (SSW). The ground underfoot turns to springy, close-cropped grass as we head up the gently inclined slope towards **Barrow Door**, the saddle between **Barrow** (455 metres) to our left and **Stile End** (447 metres) to our right. The knobbly top of **Causey Pike** (637 metres) is perfectly framed in the gap between the two.

As we gain height, the bracken-covered slopes give way to heather and bilberry, the latter providing some 'bush-tucker' for hungry walkers in the early autumn (assuming, of course, that you can beat the sheep and birds to them). On reaching **Barrow Door** (Wp.4 40M), we stick with the main path as it levels out and veers right (WSW).

We can see our way ahead clearly now - etched into the fellside by the millions of boots that have gone before us, the grey scar slices through the surrounding green to rise gently into the distance.

Ignoring several lesser paths off to the left and right, we eventually come to a T-junction with this wider track (Wp.5 51M) where we turn right.

As we climb gently and the views to our right open out, our eyes are drawn to the amazingly long and steep slope across the valley. This is the southern face of **Grisedale Pike**. (You'll be pleased to know that we don't have to venture on to this side of the mountain; our route up follows the south-west ridge.)

That 'shack' at the bottom of the long slope is **Force Crag Mine** - a lead, zinc and *baryte* mine which has been worked intermittently since Elizabethan times. A lead vein was located at **Coledale** head in 1578, although concentrated mining didn't start until the early part of the 19th century. The last attempt to extract ore was made by the New Coledale

Mining Company in 1984, but the firm left in 1990 after a large collapse flooded part of the workings. The mine was declared a Scheduled Ancient Monument in 2003 and public safety work was carried out on the buildings. The National Trust now runs occasional tours of the site.

Our way ahead curves round to the left as we start climbing up a narrower and steeper section of path with **Long Comb** to our right. Trudging uphill, with a sense of urgency in every step as the ground beneath our feet refuses to stay put, we breathe a sigh of relief when we reach the saddle between **Causey Pike** to our left and **Sail** to our right (Wp.6 98M). Plonking ourselves wearily on the grass, we sit and enjoy the fresh views to the south, including the **High Stile** range, prominent to the south west, and, beyond that, mighty **Pillar**.

So, what looks like the most difficult route ahead now? The one to the right? Well, that must be our's then. Off we go! Moaning and groaning, we plod slowly up the steep, stony path to our right. But our complaints are tempered by the amazing vista being unveiled to our left. **High Stile** has disappeared temporarily, but beyond the mountains of the **Newlands** Round, gently carved from the Skiddaw Slates, are the bigger and craggier monsters of the **Scafell** range, hacked uncompromisingly from the Borrowdale Volcanics.

From the unmarked top of **Sail** (Wp.7 118M), we drop to a slender saddle between **Sail** and **Crag Hill**. Although it's no less than about eight feet at its narrowest, this section of path may cause problems for vertigo sufferers in high winds; others may enjoy the slight sense of exposure.

The route up to Crag Hill

The climb up from the saddle is a little more interesting and challenging than the previous ascents of the day. Sometimes on bare rock, you may need your hands as we scramble to the top of **Crag Hill** (Wp.8 143M). There are good views of the whole of the horseshoe from the trig point and, although we are now at the highest point on the walk, we can see quite clearly that plenty more ascent awaits us on our way to the remaining tops.

There are two cairned routes leading away from the summit. We want the more prominent one to the left (SW). Shooting down this easy slope, we reach a crossroads in a dip (Wp.9 153M).

Turning right, we head down towards the pass at **Coledale Hause**. Keeping the beck on our left, we turn left at a cairn (Wp.10 173M) on to a narrower path. (The escape route, in case of emergency, can be found by ignoring this turn and continuing along the main track.) Bearing right at the next fork (Wp.11 175M), we meet up with a path coming in from our right in the pass proper. Looking left, we can see right down **Gasgale Gill** to **Crummock Water**.

Squelching our way across the soggy pass, we are faced with a choice of routes ahead (Wp.12 178M). So, what looks like the most difficult route? The one to the left? You've guessed it - that's our's! (Of course, you could turn right here to cut the corner and head straight up on to **Grisedale Pike**, but it'd be a real shame to miss out **Hopegill Head**.)

Scree-covered, the ascent looks pretty tough from here, but it's all over in a flash and we soon encounter level ground as we join the ridge path coming in from the right (Wp.13 203M). Just two minutes more and we're at the airy summit of **Hopegill Head**, to be greeted by views opening out to the north. Retracing our steps to the junction at Wp.13, we bear left to follow the gently descending path on the edge of the fell. Take some time to look behind at awesome **Hobcarton Crag**, the dark, inaccessible cliffs that are home to the rare red alpine catchfly.

The ridge path dips slightly before we begin the final big climb of the day - up to **Grisedale Pike**. It's not the steepest ascent of the route, but it'll seem rather long after all the climbing we've already done. Heading up on a wonderful ridge path, we enjoy a great sense of true mountain walking and, from the top, marked by only a small cairn sitting atop a rocky outcrop, take in tremendous views in all directions (Wp.14 236M). We drop down from the summit, taking care to bear right when we see two rusty fence posts close together on our left (Wp.15 239M). The route is not obvious in misty conditions.

Descending from Grisedale Pike

Initially, the way down looks pretty tricky and, initially, it is. But as we pick our way carefully down the shattered rock and set our sights a little further ahead, a wonderful section of ridge path is visible that beckons us on. Once down on to this narrow but safe section, things get much easier. The path then bears right, away from the main ridge after ten minutes (Wp.16 276M) to drop to another very pleasant looking, grassy ridge.

Crossing a stile (Wp.17 310M) close to the edge of the forest, we begin our descent to **Braithwaite**. Zigzagging our way down through bracken and sweet-smelling foxgloves, we reach the road at a car park (Wp.18 320M). (GPS reception is poor along this road.) Turning right, we stride down the road to take the first turning on the right (Wp.19 328M). Crossing the bridge over **Coledale Beck**, we stroll along this lane back to the white church where we started the day (Wp.1 330M), and ready now for a well-deserved drink and a bite to eat at one of the village pubs.

This short, low-level walk starts with a gentle stroll through pleasant mixed woodland just above **Crummock Water** where we're likely to see lots of red squirrels. We then cross farmland before returning to the parking area via a level path at the base of the fells.

Cumbria is one of the last strongholds of the native red squirrels, which have been replaced in most of England and Wales by the grey, introduced from North America in 1876. Because greys breed rapidly with two litters a year, and are better able to survive a severe winter due to their extra body fat, they out-compete the native species, particularly in lowland deciduous woodland. They have been known to displace the much cuter reds completely within seven years of arrival in a wood. Red squirrels are also more susceptible to certain diseases and find it less easy to adapt when hedgerows and woodland are destroyed. There are many projects throughout the region, mostly run in conjunction with Red Alert North West, to monitor and protect the species.

(* in nearby **Loweswater** village)

Access by car: The walk starts from the parking area next to **Lanthwaite Green Farm** near **Crummock Water** (GR NY158208). If you are driving to the start of the walk, from **Cockermouth** follow the B5289 south towards **Buttermere**, taking a left turn after 6.0 miles. The parking area, which has a phone box in it, is on your right 1.25 miles after this junction.

Access by bus: In the summer, the 77/77A (Honister Rambler) passes **Lanthwaite Green** Farm on its circular route between **Keswick** and **Buttermere**, as does the 263 (Ennerdale Rambler) from **Maryport** to **Buttermere** and **Bowness Knott**. The rest of the year, the area is served by a dial-a-ride service (see appendix).

From the parking area (Wp.1 0M), we turn left to walk along the road for 120 yards until, just after the farm buildings, we turn left at a footpath sign to cross a stone stile beside a locked gate (Wp.2 1M).

We snake our way between walls and fences before going through a kissing-gate on our left (Wp3. 5M) to cross the field towards the woods, keeping a drystone wall on our right. We enter **Lanthwaite Wood** via another gate (Wp.4 6M) and then follow the track as it bears slightly left. As the path swings round to the right, the trees thin and we get a good view left to **Crummock Water** and, on the other side of the lake, the steep-sided, brooding **Mellbreak** (512 metres). (GPS reception is intermittent at best in **Lanthwaite**

Woods.) The woods are home to a large population of red squirrels. You'll be unlucky if you don't see at least one or two foraging for food, scampering up and down the trees or chasing each other through the fallen leaves. You may also see deer while wandering between the trees, as well as a variety of birdlife. As another track comes in from the left, we keep straight ahead and then bear right at a fork (Wp.5 23M), heading slightly uphill. Marching easily along this clear track, we keep straight ahead at a crossing of paths and then turn right when we reach the road (Wp.6 29M).

Watch carefully for the next turning – it's easy to miss. We pass **Scale Hill** holiday cottages on our left, followed by a cottage called **Watching How** on our right. Almost 200 yards beyond this cottage, there is a stile and footpath sign slightly back from the road to the right and partly hidden by the trees (Wp.7 33M). Over this stile, we gain access to a narrow path through the woods. (GPS reception is poor in the woods.) We weave in and out of the trees on this path for 40 yards before turning right onto a wider, grassy path crossing our way (Wp.8), following it until we take a faint, muddy path heading down through the trees to the left (Wp.9 35M), sliding down the slope on a messy combination of mud and fallen leaves.

At the bottom, we gingerly cross the wobbly, lop-sided stile and plank bridge and then walk across the field ahead, keeping a row of oak trees on our left. It's important to stick to the public right of way across this private land. Having reached a wall, we keep it on our left until we come to a wooden stile (Wp.10). Crossing this, we ascend the field to a drystone wall ahead, keeping a fence on our immediate left. Over the wall via a stile, we bear left to pick up a clear, grassy track. Coming to a road, we go straight across and through a gate to cross a footbridge, after which we bear slightly left to go through another gate (Wp.11 46M). Having had to practically wade our way through the mud near the gate, we now plod up the hill with a fence/wall on our right. We're heading for that horrendously steep ladder stile at the top of the enclosure. Having crossed it (Wp.12 50M), we turn right along a clear path through the bracken at the base of **Whiteside**, really striding out now as we follow the line of the wall along easy, mostly level ground, ignoring all paths off to our left.

After fifteen minutes of easy striding from the stile, our route curves right for us to cross **Liza Beck** via a wide bridge (Wp.13 67M) and continue straight ahead on a faint path until we reach a vehicle track (Wp.14) where we turn left. On the relatively level and low-lying ground to our left between **Crummock Water** and the steep slopes of **Grasmoor**, it's possible to make out the remains of hut circles and boundary walls that are thought to be part of a late Iron Age farming settlement.

Crossing Liza Beck (Wp.13)

There are few such archaeological sites in the Lake District – others include **Threlkeld Knotts** and **Millrigg** in the **Kentmere Valley**. On reaching the road, we turn left, and it's a quick 120 yards back to the car park (Wp.1).

This lovely, almost effortless walk makes use of bridleways south of **Loweswater**. There is a gentle climb near the beginning of the route, but after that, we're on a wide, easy-to-follow track with some great views. The return is via a pleasant woodland path beside the lake.

| 1/2 | 2 H | 5.5 miles/8.9km | 270m 270m | 4* |

*in nearby **Loweswater** village

Access by car: the walk starts from the **Maggie's Bridge** car park near **Loweswater** (GR NY134210). You will normally need to drive to the start of the walk as it is not served by a regular bus. From **Cockermouth**, follow the B5289 south towards **Buttermere**. Ignore all roads off, even when you reach the left turn for **Buttermere** after 6.0 miles. You continue for another 1.65 miles beyond this junction along a winding and undulating road. After passing a phone box on the edge of Loweswater village, take the second turn on your left. The car park is just at the bottom of this dead-end lane.

Access by bus: the area is served by a dial-a-ride service (see appendix).

Carling Knott from the track to
High Nook Farm

Starting from the car park (Wp.1 0M), we ignore the signposted path that goes to **Watergate Farm** and instead head out of the car park in the opposite direction, turning right after a few yards (Wp.2 1M). Going through a gate, we stroll along the clear track up to **High Nook Farm**.

Having gone through one gate (Wp.3 10M), we walk through the yard, passing the farmhouse on the left and then through another gate. Ignoring a path that seems to cross the stream, we keep to the path next to the drystone wall on our left. With **Highnook Beck** accompanying us and the slopes of the low-lying western fells willing us on, we shoot up this first uphill section on a clear track.

We go through a gate in a wall (Wp.4 16M) and, ignoring a path off to the left some 60 yards beyond the gate, we start heading slightly downhill. Bearing right at a fork (Wp.5 19M) we squelch our way across some soggy ground down to a small wooden bridge across **Highnook Beck** (Wp.6 21M).

Once across, our path bears right for us to climb gently, turning our backs on the fells that seem to have been beckoning us since **High Nook Farm** and facing the more dramatic mountains on the other side of the **Lorton Valley** – **Whiteside** (707 metres) and **Grasmoor** (852 metres).

After ten minutes of fairly gentle uphill work, our path levels off slightly and we reach the edge of a dark conifer plantation. A few minutes on, the level is soon replaced by more uphill work, made harder by the unnatural silence of the forest, broken only by the sound the wind through the trees and the occasional harsh cawing of crows. But the oppressiveness suddenly ends as we go through a gate (Wp.7 40M) and the views open out to the **Irish Sea** far ahead of us, and, before long, we also catch glimpses of **Loweswater** through the trees.

We amble along the lovely grassy track as it drops down to cross **Holme Beck** (Wp.8 48M) and then continues its undulating way around the side of **Burnbank Fell**. From the beginning of the 13th century until the 17th century, when **Loweswater** was a chapel to **St Bees Abbey**, coffins would be carried on horseback along this bridleway to **Lamplugh** and then on to **St Bees** on the coast. Despite its morbid beginnings, it's a delightful path and we have the added benefit of a well-placed bench just to the right of it (Wp.9 53M), which affords some wonderful views down **Loweswater** and **Crummock Water**.

Beyond the bench, we climb gently to the first of several gates (Wp.10 60M). It's mostly downhill from here as we pass through another two gates. When the wide track swings sharply to the left (Wp.11 72M), we leave it by turning right over a ladder stile near a signpost.

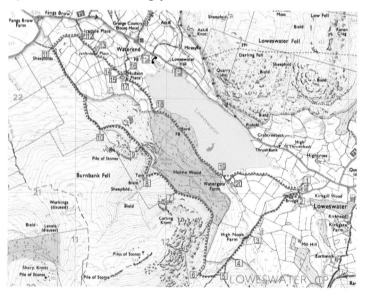

Heading towards 'Loweswater via Hudson Place', we slowly descend, keeping close to the wall on the right. At a junction with a surfaced lane, we turn right (Wp.12 78M) and then right again after the gate leading to the dismal-looking, but wonderfully situated grey cottages of **Jenkinson Place**.

After crossing a stile by a gate (Wp.13 83M), we find ourselves on a faint path through the grass heading down towards a gate and then following a row of gnarled trees and bushes on our left.

We cross a double stile at another gate (Wp.14 86M) to head towards the buildings at **Hudson Place**. Just before the buildings, we cross a stile beside a gate on the left (Wp.15) and bear right beyond the gate to gain access to a surfaced lane after another gate (Wp.16).

Turning right along the lane, we pass in front of the whitewashed buildings of **Hudson Place**. Two gates mark the end of the lane and we go through the left-hand one (Wp.17 89M).

Loweswater

We have great views of **Loweswater** straight ahead. At the bottom of this narrow path, we cross the gate/stile to access the lake-shore track through **Holme Woods** (Wp.18 93M).

The mixed woodland here is full of life compared with the top of the forest, which is given over mostly to tightly-packed conifers; birdlife is rich, and in spring, the forest floor is carpeted with wildflowers. We saunter through the woods, reluctantly leaving them at a gate (Wp.19 111M), a few yards beyond which we turn left to cross a tiny stream on a narrow path. We then turn left again at a vehicle-wide track (Wp.20 113M) and follow this back to the car park (Wp.1 120M).

Mellbreak (512 metres) is the brooding fell that looms darkly over **Crummock Water** and **Loweswater** village. It stands alone, isolated from its nearest neighbours by the horrendous bogs of **Mosedale**. The origin of the name **Mellbreak** is not certain, although it may be a combination of the Welsh word *moel* - meaning bare hill - and the old Norse word *brekka*, meaning hillslope, often referring to a hill whose slopes drop down to the water's edge, as **Mellbreak's** do.

Our route heads first into bleak **Mosedale**, but then goes straight up the western side of the fell long before we encounter any seriously damp ground. The path is very steep, but the climb is relatively short. Once we've gained the lonely summit plateau, the going is much easier. The route down is via **Black Beck** and **Scale Beck** and then **Crummock Water's** lakeshore path.

Access by car: The walk starts from the phone box on the edge of **Loweswater** village (GR NY143211), where there is parking for a few cars. You will need to drive to the start of the walk as it is not served by a regular bus. From **Cockermouth**, follow the B5289 south towards **Buttermere**. Ignore all roads off, even when you reach the left turn for **Buttermere** after 6.0 miles. Continue for another 1.3 miles beyond this junction along a winding and undulating road until you reach the phone box.

Access by bus: the area is served by a dial-a-ride service (see appendix).

We start the walk by heading down the road to the left of the phone box (Wp.1 0M) towards the **Kirkstile Inn**. The steep-sided, dark fell on our left is **Mellbreak**, looming menacingly over what is otherwise a picture of rural tranquility - sheep and cows grazing in the fields, farmers going about their business and pretty cottages dotted about the landscape.

The brooding Mellbreak

Drawing level with the church, we turn left (Wp.2 2M) and then immediately right. As we pass a whitewashed farmhouse on our right (5M), the asphalt lane disappears and we find we are walking along a stony track instead. Going through a gate at the edge of a small forested area (Wp.3 13M), we bear right along the clear track with a drystone wall/fence on our right.

We soon leave the trees behind and are strolling through the open dale with **Mosedale Beck** babbling below us on our right. A peaceful spot even in the summer, **Mosedale** is oppressively lonely in the winter when walkers know to

keep away from the quagmire that mars the head of the valley.

Sixteen minutes beyond the gate at Wp.3, we bear left at a cairn (Wp.4 29M) on to a narrow path through the bracken. We gain very little height at first as we walk almost parallel with the bridleway we've just left.

Joining another path as it comes in from the right (Wp.5 34M), we climb more noticeably on a wider track. About a quarter-of-a-mile ahead, you should be able to see the solitary **Mosedale Holly Tree**.

This is said to be the only lone tree in Britain marked on Ordnance Survey maps. Exactly 120 yards after Wp.5, we turn sharp left straight up the fellside on a path through the bracken (Wp.6). The start of the path is not marked by a cairn and, in the summer, is well-camouflaged by bracken, so we need to keep a careful eye out for it.

There's no denying it - this is a very steep path, and it can also be extremely loose in places. Soon after the only rocky section on the ascent, we bear left at a faint fork (Wp.7 49M). **Great Borne** (or Herdus) is visible just to the left of **Hen Comb** directly across the valley from us if we turn round to 'admire the view'; taking a much-needed break from this exhausting climb.

The path becomes narrower as we weave our way up the fell. At last - the pink-tinged scree slopes of **Grasmoor** suddenly appear ahead of us, meaning that the summit plateau must be close by now. Just a few weary strides later and we reach a T-junction with **Mellbreak's** main summit path (Wp.8 61M). Turning left, we stride out along the sometimes damp top with magnificent views across to **Grasmoor**. The dark gullies on the 852-metre mountain's western face look positively nightmarish to us mere walkers from here - only serious scramblers are likely to attempt **Lorton Gully** or **Grasmoor End Arête**.

Bearing left at a fork in the path (Wp.9 67M), we climb easily to the cairn (Wp.10 70M). So, this is the top! Or is it? Or maybe it's that other cairn just to our right.

Actually, the true summit - although there's only three metres in it - is about two-thirds of a mile away to the south-east. But these two cairns at the northern end are well placed for views down to **Loweswater** and across to the

Scottish hills.

From the first cairn, we turn right and walk across to the other, slightly higher cairn, from which we get a better view down **Lorton Vale** and across to **Grasmoor**.

Grasmo

Turning right, we take the wider of the two paths in front of us (SSE). It's hard to believe that this broad, featureless plateau stretching out ahead of us belongs to that steep-sided beast we were gaping at from **Loweswater** village at the beginning of the walk.

Crummock Water and Buttermere

Striding out across the heathery top, we soon pass the fork at Wp.9 and the path we came up on (Wp.8) before we begin climbing again. There are one or two boggy patches to negotiate, but otherwise the way up is easy.

The true summit (Wp.11 93M) is marked by a tiny cairn to the left of the path. Straight ahead of us now as we begin our descent is the **High Stile** range, the first knobble being the summit of **Red Pike** (see Walk 36). Our descent is very steep in places, but with those views of **Buttermere** and **Crummock Water** lifting our spirits, you'll feel like running down the grassy path ahead of us.

Ignoring all paths off, we keep straight ahead until a fence blocks further progress (Wp.12 119M). Turning right, with the fence on our left, we follow the narrow path to a stile near a gate (Wp.13 124M). We cross and shoot straight down the slope with a fence on our right to reach a T-junction near a gate (Wp.14 128M) where we turn left.

With **Crummock Water** beckoning us, we follow **Black Beck** downstream. The tree-lined ravine to our right hides **Scale Force**, which has the longest drop of any Lake District waterfall (38 metres). It's not easy to spot in summer when the trees have leaves on them, but it is quite a sight in the winter. Wordsworth described it as a, "fine chasm, with a lofty, though but slender, fall of water".

Dropping down to, but not crossing, a small wooden bridge (139M), we keep the water - now **Scale Beck** - on our right. We soon find ourselves right at the water's edge, using stepping stones to get to a small gate. Going through, we pass a sheepfold and then, as we ignore another bridge to our right, we bear left away from the beck (Wp.15 155M).

Crummock Water

Before long, we are strolling by the lakeside. This is a delightful path, made better by recent repairs that mean we no longer get our feet wet across the sometimes boggy ground.

As we approach the northern end of the lake - almost 1.3 miles after leaving the beck at Wp.15, we leave the main path by turning left through the bracken (WNW) for 60 yards (Wp.16 192M). On reaching a clear path, we turn right and follow it up to a wall and then along the edge of an old wood.

Turning right to go through a gate just after a cottage (Wp.17 207M), we walk down the enclosed path to a surfaced lane near more cottages (Wp.18 209M). We turn left here and then left at the road. At the next junction, we turn left again (Wp.19 211M) to amble along the road back to the church and the **Kirkstile Inn** (Wp.2 218M), which serves good bar meals. Turning right, the phone box (Wp.1) is now just a two-minute stroll away.

35 HAY STACKS

At 597 metres, **Hay Stacks** is far from being one of the Lake District's mightiest mountains and yet it has a special quality that makes it a favourite of many walkers, including Alfred Wainwright. It was here that his ashes were scattered after his death in 1991.

So, what made him love this "shaggy and undisciplined terrier" of a mountain? "You have to climb to the top and wander about to understand," he wrote. "Above the wall of defending crags is a fascinating landscape, a confusing labyrinth of miniature peaks and tors, of serpentine tracks, of lovely tarns, of crags and screes, of marshes and streams, of surprises around every corner, with magnificent views all around. For a man trying to forget a persistent worry, the top of Haystacks is a complete cure."

The climb from **Scarth Gap** to the summit is very steep - almost a scramble at times - so it's best not to attempt this walk in snow or ice unless you have full winter equipment.

Access by car: the walk starts from **Gatesgarth Farm** (GR NY194150) on the **Buttermere** side of **Honister Pass**. Taking the B5289 **Borrowdale** road, it is 11 miles south-west of **Keswick** or 12 miles south-east of **Cockermouth**. There is pay and display parking at the farm.

Access by bus: In the summer, the 77/77A (Honister Rambler) passes **Gatesgarth Farm** on its circular route between **Keswick** and **Buttermere,** but there are no buses in the winter (see appendix).

Starting from the car park at **Gatesgarth Farm** (Wp.1 0M), we cross the road to go through the walkers' gates, signposted 'Buttermere and Ennerdale'. Having strolled across the flat area at the SE end of **Buttermere**, we go through a gate (Wp.2 12M) and head uphill to the right of a fence enclosing a small group of trees, staying with the fence when it turns to the left at a junction of paths (Wp.3 17M). As we climb relentlessly, first on a constructed path, we'll no doubt need to stop occasionally to catch our breath. And we've got a good excuse as we head up to **Scarth Gap** - pausing to admire the wonderful and ever-changing views of **Buttermere** behind us (see picture on next page).

High Crag from Gatesgarth Farm

Just after the path levels out to give us a brief respite from the uphill slog, we

Buttermere, as seen on the way up to Scarth Gap

pass through a gap in a tumbledown drystone wall (Wp.4 49M), beyond which the track becomes boulder-strewn.

We struggle upwards - always careful not to twist an ankle on the rocks underfoot - until, finally, we reach the pass at **Scarth Gap** (Wp.5 65M). This is marked by a large cairn to our left; the path to the right heads up on to the craggy **High Stile** range (see Walk 36).

If you are using walking poles, you should probably put them away at this point as you'll need your hands on the more difficult sections as we turn left to start the climb up to **Hay Stacks**. The path up this western ridge of the mountain is relatively short, but the scrambling slows us down.

Our route is obvious, and although there are one or two forks along the way, whichever option you take to pick your way slowly through the crags will bring you out at the same place.

After the climb, we head for the large cairn slightly to the left for superb panoramic views (Wp.6 98M).

Subsequent timings do not take any detours into consideration, but you're bound to wander away from the path at times to admire the views, or simply to explore **Hay Stacks'** many nooks and crannies. So, what exactly can we see? Well, as we were climbing, the dark, craggy mountain behind us (SW) is **Pillar** (892 metres); the more pyramid-like one with steep scree slopes (NW) is **High Crag** (744 metres), and as we head across the top of **Hay Stacks**, the dome-like **Great Gable** is visible (SE 899 metres).

The view down the gully towards Buttermere

Staying on the north side of the ridge, we now clamber down and then up to the next large cairn (Wp.7 104M). From here, we stick with the clearer path on the northern side of **Hay Stacks**, ignoring a path off to the right.

After a few short but scrambly descents, we reach **Innominate Tarn** (Wp.8 115M), sticking with the clear path to the left of this picturesque puddle. We skirt the water's edge and then swing left to descend and curve around the base of a crag for some stunning views down dark, steep-sided gullies towards **Buttermere**.

After fording the outlet stream from **Blackbeck Tarn** (Wp.9 126M), we climb briefly again and then turn left at a junction with another path (Wp.10).

When a grassy path comes in from the right, we keep left and start descending.

Reaching an indistinct fork (Wp.11 141M) we bear right; the left-hand, less obvious branch heads steeply downhill. Heading straight towards the ugly spoil heaps of the recently reborn **Honister** slate operations, we ford **Warnscale Beck** 350 yards after the fork (Wp.12 149M) and then bear left.

Hay Stacks, left, and High Crag, from the Warnscale Beck path

200 yards after crossing the stream, we join a wider path coming in from our right (Wp.13). This now descends steeply to the valley floor and around the base of **Fleetwith Pike**. (GPS reception can be poor in this area.)

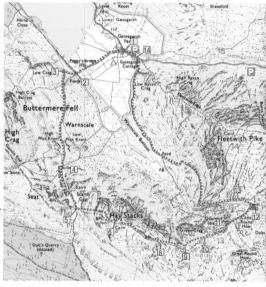

The long descent can be tiresome, but fortunately we have at least a couple of things to take our minds off the loose, rocky ground underfoot – in the early stages, **Warnscale Beck** passes through an interesting, steep-sided gully with occasional waterfalls; later on, beautiful **Buttermere**, which has been our companion for much of the walk, makes a welcome reappearance to fill the view ahead.

Reaching the road (Wp.14 205M), we turn left to stroll the 150 yards back to our start point at the car park.

The **High Stile** range of mountains - **Red Pike** (755 metres), **High Stile** (807 metres) and **High Crag** (744 metres) - lies between **Buttermere** and **Ennerdale**. Taking in a climb beside the longest waterfall in the Lake District and then returning via a relaxing lakeside path, the middle part of this tough day consists of a superb ridge walk with stunning views of some of the area's highest mountains.

It's probably best to avoid this route in misty conditions as it's easy to take a wrong turning. There is also a very slight risk of vertigo on some of the ridge paths, especially in windy conditions. The ridge is never particularly narrow though, so walkers who don't have a head for heights can easily move away from exposed edges.

5 | 4¾ H | 8½ miles/13.7km | 915m 915m | ⚠ | ↻ | 🍴 3

Access by car: The walk starts from the Lake District National Park car park at **Buttermere** on the B5289, about 13 miles south-west of **Keswick** or 10 miles south-east of **Cockermouth**.

Access by bus: Buttermere is served by the N°77/77A Honister Rambler circular bus route from Easter until the end of October and the N°263 Ennerdale Rambler (see appendix).

Leaving the car park (Wp.1 0M), we bear right to keep the white-washed **Fish Inn** on our right as we pick up the wide lane that heads down to the lake. The lane turns a sharp left and then, just before it does a sharp right, we leave it by turning right through a gate (Wp.2 3M) towards **Scale Bridge** and **Scale Force**.

The footbridge near Crummock Water

After crossing **Buttermere Dubs** via the humpback **Scale Bridge** (Wp.3 10M), we turn right along an obvious track. Several streams coming down from the fells to our left drain into this flat, marshy area between **Buttermere** and **Crummock Water** - but the well-

Crummock Water

positioned path means we're able to keep our boots dry for the time being.

As we reach the eastern end of **Crummock Water**, we ignore a faint path off to our right (18M) and continue along the increasingly rough track.

There are now one or two soggy patches to cross, but there are consolations to be had – our climb is relatively easy at this stage of the day, we have **Crummock Water** to keep us company and we've got a magnificent day of fell-walking ahead of us.

The gentle gradient comes to an abrupt end as we reach and go through a gate (Wp.4 49M). There's a bridge across **Scale Beck** visible below us; it's worth popping down to it, as it provides us with our only chance today of seeing **Scale Force**, which has the longest drop of any Lake District waterfall (38 metres). Wordsworth described it as a "fine chasm, with a lofty, though but slender, fall of water".

Scale Force

From the bridge, we head back towards the gate at Wp.4 and, just before we reach it, turn right up a constructed pathway. Accompanied by the sound of **Scale Force**, hidden in its damp, dark gorge just off to our right, we climb steeply, losing the constructed path just before **Scale Beck** comes into sight.

There are one or two rocky sections to negotiate now and, soon after clambering up the hardest of these, we reach a fork (Wp.5 68M). One path continues along the beck, but we bear left up a steep, rough track that climbs away from the valley bottom. It's important to be alert here because there are one or two sheep trods through the heather that might lead us astray. Reaching the top of a small, but steep-sided, red-soiled gully, one of these red herring paths heads off to the right (76M) - but we must keep straight on ahead, still climbing. Forty yards beyond this junction, we veer right to join up with a cairned path heading in a generally SE direction (Wp.6 78M). Route finding gets a little easier now as we follow the clear, cairned path and, thankfully, the gradient eases as we approach the top of this open, heathery slope.

Red Pike from Lingcomb Edge

Reaching **Lingcomb Edge** (Wp.7 98M), we bear right with the rounded top of **Red Pike** looming large ahead. With slopes falling away steeply down to **Crummock Water** and **Buttermere** to our left, this is a wonderful route on to the fell, assuming, of course that you don't suffer from vertigo. (If you do, just head a little to the right and you'll discover a flatter, broader expanse of grass.)

The ascent is relatively easy until we reach the base of **Red Pike** proper where we find ourselves battling our way up a very loose, steep path. The fact that **Ennerdale** has appeared to our right barely registers as we struggle to gain a decent foothold. But the battle is short-lived; we soon arrive at the summit cairn and shelter (Wp.8 129M) where we can rest a while and enjoy the views.

Crummock Water from Red Pike

The ridge stretches on invitingly ahead of us, rising to a high point of 807 metres just three-quarters of a mile away. It's easy to get lost on these fells in misty conditions, so if the cloud does descend, consider descending the NE side of **Red Pike** towards **Bleaberry Tarn**. (The start of the path is marked by a cairn). This, however, is one of the most severely eroded footpaths in the Lake District, so care must be taken if you choose this option.

To continue along the ridge from the top of **Red Pike**, we head south along a faint path on the eastern edge of the fell for 175 yards and then veer SE to drop down on to a more obvious path that follows the top of **Chapel Crags**. We now have a line of rusty fenceposts accompanying us; these old border markers are never far away as we make our way along the ridge, and can prove a useful navigation aid in hill fog.

As we stride out along a short, but welcome section of level walking, the ground to our left drops away steeply to **Bleaberry Tarn**. The deep *corrie* in which it is couched was once described by Romantic poet Robert Southey as

Red Pike from High Stile

the crater of an extinct volcano, although we now know that it is glacial in origin. Looking back, it soon becomes apparent how **Red Pike** got its name. The red scree exists because most of the fell is composed of an igneous intrusion, the **Ennerdale** *granophyre*.

We soon begin climbing again – this time on to **High Stile**, the highest point on the walk. The path passes close to a cairn sitting on top of a group of rocks. This may look like the summit, but the true top is marked by a large cairn another 195 yards to the east (Wp.9 149M).

From here, there are magnificent views in all directions. All four of the Lake District's 3,000-foot fells are visible; and **Pillar** dominates the scene to the south.

Looking to the south-east, in the general direction of **Great Gable** and the **Scafells**, our next section of ridge path can be seen lying almost 100 metres below **High Stile**. Finding our way on to it can be easier said than done, especially in fog. What we definitely <u>don't</u> want to do is head along the clearly cairned path to our left (NE); instead, we walk across to the eastern edge of the fell and then bear right along a faint path that descends in a mostly southerly direction before veering SE.

We're now on the narrowest section of the entire ridge and, although it's never less than a comfortable 80 feet wide, you may want to keep away from the edge in strong winds. If we look behind we may be able to spot climbers clinging to some of the magnificent rock pinnacles that crowd the eastern face of **High Stile**.

Heading onto High Crag

The summit of High Crag

Picking our way along the often rocky path, it is with heavy heart that we approach the final top of the day - **High Crag** - knowing that we are nearing the end of this magnificent ridge.

From the summit cairn (Wp.10 181M), we plunge steeply down the SE side of the mountain, first on loose scree and then on a constructed, zigzagging path. Coming out of the final zigzag - as the constructed path heads straight down into a grassy depression - we veer left along a very faint, grassy path (Wp.11 203M). We keep to this path for only 67 yards; just before it passes to the right of a large boulder we turn left (E) across the pathless fellside to pass the boulder on our right (Wp.12 204M). There is nothing to guide us for the next 70 yards, although we want to ensure that we keep about 100 yards from that white post on the rocks ahead and to our right. Eventually, we'll see a tumbledown drystone wall ahead; making a beeline for that, we pick up a path running alongside it (Wp.13 206M).

Turning right, we keep the sometimes scant remains of the wall on our left to pick our way carefully down the loose, rocky path until we reach a T-junction with another track (Wp.14 224M). We turn left to continue our downhill journey at a much gentler gradient and on a better path. Crossing a small stream via a plank bridge (243M), we reach the edge of a small area of woodland to our right. We follow the fence dividing us from the woodland until it makes a sharp right turn at a junction of paths (Wp.15 245M). Keeping straight ahead here - downhill towards the lake - we turn left when we reach the next path junction (Wp.16 248M) to end the day with a lovely lakeside stroll.

Soon after entering the woods (where GPS reception is poor), we come to a fork in the path where we can take either branch. Emerging from the woods at the western end of the lake, we keep to the level, gravel path as it veers right to cross two footbridges. At the end of this path (Wp.17 278M), we turn left through a gate at a National Trust signpost and follow the winding lane back to the village with its selection of pubs, café and ice-cream shop - and the car park (Wp.1 285M).

Please see the notes on GPS and using these waypoints on page 20.

1
AIRA FORCE
No reliable GPS coverage

2
HALLIN FELL

Wp	Zo	E	N
1	NY	43589	19226
2	NY	43633	19254
3	NY	43356	20422
4	NY	42674	19979
5	NY	43172	19373
6	NY	43509	19374
7	NY	43302	19817
8	NY	43566	19805
9	NY	43604	19467
10	NY	43556	19170
11	NY	43605	19009
12	NY	43460	18894
13	NY	43431	18673
14	NY	43418	18392
15	NY	43426	19071

3
POOLEY BRIDGE TO HOWTOWN

Wp	Zo	E	N
1	NY	47039	24353
2	NY	47271	24466
3	NY	47462	24334
4	NY	47888	23580
5	NY	48288	22729
6	NY	48250	22256
7	NY	47319	21987
8	NY	44563	19980
9	NY	44369	19855
10	NY	44315	19898

4
GOWBARROW

Wp	Zo	E	N
1	NY	40061	20047
2	NY	39870	20473
3	NY	40065	20844
4	NY	39895	21567
5	NY	40761	21816
6	NY	41446	21762
7	NY	41283	20866
8	NY	40144	20402

5
PIKEAWASSA

Wp	Zo	E	N
1	NY	43569	19163
2	NY	43581	19130
3	NY	43791	19059
4	NY	44316	19413
5	NY	44038	18565
6	NY	44035	18122
7	NY	44098	17813
8	NY	44131	17672
9	NY	44700	16920
10	NY	44676	17327
11	NY	44565	17611
12	NY	44547	18523
13	NY	44527	18656
14	NY	44483	18659
15	NY	44483	19011
16	NY	44443	19398

6
BOREDALE ROUND - PLACE FELL & BEDA FELL

Wp	Zo	E	N
1	NY	42773	18592
2	NY	42596	18538
3	NY	42493	18668
4	NY	41810	18400
5	NY	41337	17837
6	NY	40558	16957
7	NY	40681	16642
8	NY	40754	16475
9	NY	40863	15737
10	NY	41881	15836
11	NY	42886	17155
12	NY	42855	17601
13	NY	43025	18598

7
LOADPOT HILL

Wp	Zo	E	N
1	NY	44315	19898
2	NY	44162	19834
3	NY	44247	19661
4	NY	44482	19007
5	NY	44448	18687
6	NY	44554	18375
7	NY	44516	18082
8	NY	44570	17612
9	NY	44714	17240
10	NY	45401	17128
11	NY	45560	17253
12	NY	45685	18119
13	NY	45708	18761
14	NY	45777	18907
15	NY	46079	19797
16	NY	47885	22221
17	NY	48245	22251
18	NY	48298	22730
19	NY	47278	24463
20	NY	47034	24357

8
HIGH STREET FROM HARTSOP

Wp	Zo	E	N
1	NY	40997	12997
2	NY	41591	12541
3	NY	42550	10388
4	NY	42668	10279
5	NY	43147	9997
6	NY	43647	10239
7	NY	44080	11052
8	NY	43976	12175
9	NY	43787	12670
10	NY	43616	12849
11	NY	42211	13795
12	NY	40764	15620
13	NY	40730	15623
14	NY	40518	14605
15	NY	40658	14050
16	NY	40592	13197

9
LOW RIGG

Wp	Zo	E	N
1	NY	30638	22485
2	NY	30848	23030
3	NY	30782	23212
4	NY	30796	23423
5	NY	30837	23591
6	NY	30697	23850
7	NY	30558	23567
8	NY	30612	22514

10
HIGH RIGG

Wp	Zo	E	N
1	NY	30632	22481
2	NY	30860	21998
3	NY	30939	21112
4	NY	31143	20715
5	NY	31506	20205
6	NY	31625	19567
7	NY	31715	20463
8	NY	30714	22500

11

SHEFFIELD PIKE

Wp	Zo	E	N
1	NY	38674	18892
2	NY	38754	18687
3	NY	38381	18680
4	NY	37877	18554
5	NY	37576	18386
6	NY	37197	18551
7	NY	36306	18251
8	NY	36911	18179
9	NY	36309	18165
10	NY	36240	18181
11	NY	35931	17960
12	NY	36186	17675
13	NY	36250	17394
14	NY	36321	17385
15	NY	36534	17411
16	NY	38138	17050
17	NY	38680	17381
18	NY	38738	18527

12

LANTY'S TARN & RED TARN

Wp	Zo	E	N
1	NY	38631	16911
2	NY	38407	16776
3	NY	38305	16671
4	NY	38203	16464
5	NY	38383	16364
6	NY	38516	16338
7	NY	38516	16287
8	NY	38331	16273
9	NY	37913	16174
10	NY	37061	16035
11	NY	36477	16278
12	NY	36526	16392
13	NY	35930	15534
14	NY	35154	15377
15	NY	35042	15480
16	NY	35722	16728
17	NY	37312	16839
18	NY	37445	16868
19	NY	37791	16701
20	NY	37943	16872

13

HELVELLYN FROM THIRLMERE

Wp	Zo	E	N
1	NY	31673	16846
2	NY	31834	16857
3	NY	31976	16710
4	NY	33211	15683
5	NY	34171	15156

6	NY	34290	14509
7	NY	32776	13554
8	NY	32685	13628

14

HELVELLYN FROM GLENRIDDING

Wp	Zo	E	N
1	NY	38530	16908
2	NY	38129	17003
3	NY	36440	17395
4	NY	35214	16585
5	NY	33940	16859
6	NY	33749	15544
7	NY	34173	15157
8	NY	34291	14501
9	NY	35194	12348
10	NY	35761	13753
11	NY	37980	15516
12	NY	38318	15680
13	NY	39052	16129

15

DEEPDALE ROUND

Wp	Zo	E	N
1	NY	39320	16132
2	NY	39051	16143
3	NY	38652	15787
4	NY	38536	15269
5	NY	37295	13983
6	NY	36919	13401
7	NY	36093	12586
8	NY	35861	12074
9	NY	35874	11747
10	NY	36899	11210
11	NY	36865	11281
12	NY	37068	11335
13	NY	39861	13279
14	NY	39986	13897
15	NY	40161	14113
16	NY	39914	14418
17	NY	40339	14575
18	NY	40443	14751
19	NY	40207	15505
20	NY	40137	15653
21	NY	40035	16012
22	NY	39802	15802

16

LONGLANDS FELL & LOWTHWAITE FELL

Wp	Zo	E	N
1	NY	28274	36749
2	NY	27756	36405
3	NY	27576	35973

4	NY	27593	35402
5	NY	27701	35159
6	NY	27833	34746
7	NY	28159	34513
8	NY	28171	34789
9	NY	27724	36174

17

LATRIGG

Wp	Zo	E	N
1	NY	26763	24122
2	NY	27432	25084
3	NY	27643	24607
4	NY	27921	24696
5	NY	28140	25218
6	NY	29560	25089
7	NY	29846	24744
8	NY	28599	24124
9	NY	27009	23806

18

HIGH PIKE

Wp	Zo	E	N
1	NY	30426	37374
2	NY	30735	37385
3	NY	31219	37301
4	NY	31854	37156
5	NY	31913	37193
6	NY	32079	37129
7	NY	32050	36903
8	NY	32011	36732
9	NY	32101	36124
10	NY	31797	35788
11	NY	31871	35004
12	NY	31798	34672
13	NY	31715	35720
14	NY	31283	36574
15	NY	30948	36560
16	NY	30452	37262

19

KNOTT FROM ORTHWAITE

Wp	Zo	E	N
1	NY	25265	33745
2	NY	25552	33212
3	NY	27386	32823
4	NY	28455	32471
5	NY	28536	32463
6	NY	28719	32393
7	NY	29618	32984
8	NY	29136	33896
9	NY	28298	33761
10	NY	27900	33428
11	NY	27323	33051
12	NY	26806	32889

20
SKIDDAW THE EASY WAY

Wp	Zo	E	N
1	NY	28076	25344
2	NY	28289	25572
3	NY	28003	26256
4	NY	27161	27528
5	NY	26687	27805
6	NY	26408	28319
7	NY	26041	29085
8	NY	26453	28316
9	NY	27623	28622
10	NY	28632	29067
11	NY	28691	29147
12	NY	28929	28963
13	NY	29375	28778
14	NY	29218	27978

21
A BLENCATHRA ROUND

Wp	Zo	E	N
1	NY	36186	30310
2	NY	36376	30569
3	NY	36338	30537
4	NY	33384	30611
5	NY	33165	29841
6	NY	33120	29820
7	NY	32786	29143
8	NY	32450	28316
9	NY	32567	28317
10	NY	32342	27709
11	NY	32442	27801
12	NY	33726	27621
13	NY	34344	27708
14	NY	34622	27877
15	NY	35088	28467
16	NY	35055	28625
17	NY	35472	29135
18	NY	36245	30109
19	NY	36367	29700
20	NY	36410	29703
21	NY	36235	30292

22
RIVER DERWENT & AROUND CASTLE CRAG

Wp	Zo	E	N
1	NY	24570	13809
2	NY	24650	13861
3	NY	25442	14056
4	NY	25551	14334
5	NY	25141	15166
6	NY	25203	16058
7	NY	25068	16543
8	NY	24900	16281
9	NY	24611	15522
10	NY	24224	14171
11	NY	24442	13848

23
WALLA CRAG

Wp	Zo	E	N
1	NY	26497	22902
2	NY	26417	22276
3	NY	26904	22025
4	NY	26773	21835
5	NY	26934	20872
6	NY	26964	20831
7	NY	27062	20715
8	NY	26994	20454
9	NY	27046	19705
10	NY	27164	19620
11	NY	27219	19763
12	NY	27638	21148
13	NY	27662	21287
14	NY	27871	21542
15	NY	28361	22111
16	NY	28279	22276
17	NY	27792	22530
18	NY	27485	22627
19	NY	27217	22928
20	NY	26819	22731
21	NY	26855	22660
22	NY	26675	22605

24
WATENDLATH & GRANGE FELL

Wp	Zo	E	N
1	NY	25659	17666
2	NY	26170	18303
3	NY	26278	18300
4	NY	26480	18335
5	NY	26792	18154
6	NY	27534	16334
7	NY	27472	16271
8	NY	26910	15967
9	NY	26596	16314
10	NY	26471	16263
11	NY	26179	16111
12	NY	25923	16562
13	NY	25846	16508
14	NY	25810	16655
15	NY	26024	17107
16	NY	26015	17706

25
GREAT GABLE

Wp	Zo	E	N
1	NY	22523	13538
2	NY	22501	13488
3	NY	21999	12651
4	NY	21954	12622
5	NY	21484	11930
6	NY	21508	11673
7	NY	21472	10714
8	NY	21428	10539
9	NY	21101	10318
10	NY	21119	10821
11	NY	21064	11996
12	NY	21136	12072
13	NY	21587	13467
14	NY	22320	13539

26
GLARAMARA & ALLEN CRAGS

Wp	Zo	E	N
1	NY	23553	12166
2	NY	24631	13230
3	NY	24723	13328
4	NY	25030	13525
5	NY	24533	11847
6	NY	24589	11617
7	NY	24777	10917
8	NY	24771	10749
9	NY	24733	10632
10	NY	24721	10560
11	NY	24597	10425
12	NY	23667	08525
13	NY	23488	08327
14	NY	23142	08532
15	NY	22962	08687
16	NY	23457	09914
17	NY	23441	10908

27
SALE FELL

Wp	Zo	E	N
1	NY	19170	30179
2	NY	19055	29961
3	NY	18631	29573
4	NY	18678	29534
5	NY	19193	29595
6	NY	19438	29664
7	NY	19915	29497
8	NY	20360	29840
9	NY	19098	30097

28
CAUSEY PIKE & BARROW

Wp	Zo	E	N
1	NY	23274	21733
2	NY	22874	21195
3	NY	22767	21184
4	NY	23111	21061
5	NY	22465	20959
6	NY	22214	20703
7	NY	21913	20838
8	NY	21891	20820
9	NY	21875	20847
10	NY	20852	20663
11	NY	20428	20477
12	NY	21145	21216
13	NY	21514	21479
14	NY	21659	21685
15	NY	22145	21658
16	NY	22164	21664
17	NY	22710	21833
18	NY	23004	22380
19	NY	23348	23070
20	NY	23321	22305

29
BUTTERMERE TO HONISTER via ROBINSON & DALE HEAD

Wp	Zo	E	N
1	NY	17367	16923
2	NY	17513	16976
3	NY	17619	17022
4	NY	17866	17131
5	NY	18592	17105
6	NY	18858	17162
7	NY	20181	16872
8	NY	20759	16107
9	NY	22304	15326
10	NY	22501	13730
11	NY	22516	13566

30
NEWLANDS ROUND

Wp	Zo	E	N
1	NY	24560	21112
2	NY	24793	21126
3	NY	24408	19860
4	NY	24027	18415
5	NY	23669	18203
6	NY	23660	17738
7	NY	23411	16234
8	NY	23077	15267
9	NY	22563	15499
10	NY	22305	15327
11	NY	21497	15738
12	NY	21512	16213
13	NY	21571	16513
14	NY	22900	18598
15	NY	22987	19347
16	NY	23102	19410
17	NY	23524	19639
18	NY	24219	20865

31
COLEDALE ROUND

Wp	Zo	E	N
1	NY	22917	23590
2	NY	22917	23185
3	NY	22720	22746
4	NY	22191	21702
5	NY	21631	21562
6	NY	20430	20476
7	NY	19837	20260
8	NY	19266	20357
9	NY	18611	20166
10	NY	18869	21071
11	NY	18866	21147
12	NY	18872	21289
13	NY	18596	22115
14	NY	19840	22545
15	NY	19895	22619
16	NY	20773	22857
17	NY	22530	23635
18	NY	22745	23781
19	NY	23019	23625

32
LANTHWAITE GREEN

Wp	Zo	E	N
1	NY	15899	20780
2	NY	15875	20882
3	NY	15678	20784
4	NY	15610	20705
5	NY	15074	21228
6	NY	14943	21559
7	NY	15084	21884
8	NY	15153	21922
9	NY	15185	21906
10	NY	15248	21932
11	NY	15431	21969
12	NY	15570	21960
13	NY	15720	21985
14	NY	15738	21988
15	NY	15755	21997
16	NY	15963	22041
17	NY	16078	21096
18	NY	15939	21099

33
ABOVE LOWESWATER

Wp	Zo	E	N
1	NY	13453	21039
2	NY	13461	21012
3	NY	12917	20547
4	NY	12718	20312
5	NY	12551	20125
6	NY	12398	20128
7	NY	12121	21014
8	NY	11799	21192
9	NY	11735	21486
10	NY	11277	21672
11	NY	10752	22535
12	NY	11075	22621
13	NY	11220	22434
14	NY	11445	22297
15	NY	11496	22251
16	NY	11553	22253
17	NY	11559	22190
18	NY	11845	21858
19	NY	12624	21170
20	NY	12745	21168

34
MELLBREAK

Wp	Zo	E	N
1	NY	14306	21105
2	NY	14145	20922
3	NY	13896	20194
4	NY	13904	19071
5	NY	14067	18697
6	NY	14156	18632
7	NY	14356	18754
8	NY	14453	18996
9	NY	14367	19327
10	NY	14307	19469
11	NY	14840	18615
12	NY	14945	17588
13	NY	14640	17517
14	NY	14654	17361
15	NY	15645	17730
16	NY	14981	19685
17	NY	14444	20296
18	NY	14425	20415
19	NY	14436	20590

35
HAY STACKS

Wp	Zo	E	N
1	NY	19444	15001
2	NY	18929	14761
3	NY	18776	14772
4	NY	18773	13763
5	NY	18924	13335

6	NY	19339	13198	**36**					
7	NY	19389	13212	**HIGH STILE RANGE**					
8	NY	19827	12969	**Wp**	**Zo**	**E**	**N**		
9	NY	20108	12923	1	NY	17411	16937		
10	NY	20332	13025	2	NY	17426	16803		
11	NY	20579	13182	3	NY	16797	16574		
12	NY	20857	13350	4	NY	15078	17139		
13	NY	20687	13418	5	NY	15012	16782		
14	NY	19563	14938	6	NY	15087	16665		
				7	NY	15563	16371		

8	NY	16052	15452
9	NY	16974	14783
10	NY	18051	13994
11	NY	18284	13751
12	NY	18335	13714
13	NY	18392	13738
14	NY	18770	13769
15	NY	18782	14776
16	NY	18709	14978
17	NY	17387	16458

A PUBLIC TRANSPORT

Buses:
The following gives a rough guide to bus times for the walks covered in
this book and is based on the summer 2005 timetable. For more precise and
up-to-date information on buses, telephone Traveline on 0870 608 2608 or
visit the website at www.traveline.org.uk

Bus N°108 (walks 1, 3, 4, 7, 11, 12, 14 and 15) from **Penrith** to **Patterdale**
also serves **Pooley Bridge** and **Glenridding**. The first bus from **Penrith** is
at 06.45 (Saturdays 07.55, Sundays 09.25) and the last bus from
Patterdale is at 17.10 (Saturdays 17.10, Sundays 17.10). Five buses per
day (four on Sundays) in each direction. No Sunday service in the winter.

Bus N° 208 (walks 1, 4, 11, 12, 14 and 15) **Keswick** to **Patterdale** also
serves **Glenridding**. This runs on summer weekends only. The first bus
from **Keswick** is at 09.25 and the last bus from **Patterdale** is at 17.10. Five
buses per day in each direction.

Bus N° 517, **Kirkstone** Rambler (walks 8, 12, 14 and 15) **Bowness** to
Glenridding also serves **Patterdale**. This runs on summer weekends only.
The first bus from **Bowness** is at 09.10 and the last bus from **Glenridding**
is at 17.10. Three buses per day in each direction.

Bus N° 555 (walk 13), **Keswick** to **Kendal** via the A591. The first bus
south from **Keswick** is at 09.30 (Sundays 10.00) and the last bus back from
the **Swirls** car park is at about 18.51 (Sundays 18.36). This bus runs
roughly every hour.

Bus N° 73/73A, **Caldbeck** Rambler (walk 21) **Keswick/Carlisle** to
Caldbeck also serves **Mungrisdale**. This infrequent service runs daily
during the school summer holidays, but only on Saturdays during the
winter. The first bus from **Keswick** is at 09.20 (the first from **Carlisle** is at
08.00) and the last bus from **Mungrisdale** is at 13.11 to **Keswick** (14.44 to
Carlisle).

Bus N°79, the **Borrowdale** Rambler (walks 22, 23, 24 and 26) **Keswick** to
Seatoller serves the B5289 **Borrowdale** road. The first bus from **Keswick**
is at 07.25 (Sundays 09.25) and the last bus from **Seatoller** is at 21.18
(Sundays 18.10). This service runs roughly every half-hour (every hour on
Sundays).

Bus N° 77/77A, Honister Rambler (walks 22, 23, 24, 25, 26, 29, 31, 32, 35
and 36) circular service from **Keswick** to **Buttermere** taking in the B5289
Borrowdale road, **Honister Pass**, **Lanthwaite Green** and **Braithwaite**.
This is a summer service only. The first bus from **Keswick** is at 09.15. The
last bus is at 17.15 from **Buttermere**, 17.27 from **Honister**, 17.35 from
Seatoller and 17.20 from **Braithwaite**. Four buses clockwise and four

buses anti-clockwise each day.

Bus N° X5 (walk 31) **Penrith** to **Workington** via **Keswick** and **Cockermouth** also stops at **Braithwaite**. The first bus from **Keswick** is at 09.10 (Sundays 09.55) and the last bus from Braithwaite to Keswick is at 23.02 (Sundays 17.59). This bus runs roughly every hour (every two hours on Sundays).

Bus N° 263, **Ennerdale** Rambler (walks 29, 32, 33, 34 and 36) **Maryport** to **Bowness Knott** also serves **Buttermere** and **Loweswater**. This is a summer service only. The only bus from Maryport is at 08.55 and the last bus from **Buttermere** is at 17.20 (16..46 from **Loweswater**).

Bus N° 949 dial-a-ride service (walks 29, 32, 33 and 36) **Cockermouth** to **Buttermere** also serves **Loweswater**. The first bus from **Cockermouth** is at 09.45 and the last bus from **Buttermere** is at 14.58. Three buses per day in each direction. No Sunday service. To book, telephone Ken Routledge Travel on 01900 822795 the day before travel.

Boats:
Keswick Launch on **Derwentwater** (walks 23 and 30). From the end of March until the end of November, boats start at 09.45 from **Keswick** and the last one arrives back in **Keswick** at 19.50 (daily). They depart every half hour. During the winter, they run on Saturdays and Sundays only, except during the school holidays when they are daily (first boat 10.30; last boat arrives back in **Keswick** at 16.20). Only three services clockwise and three services anti-clockwise during the winter. Timetable subject to alteration without notice. For full details, phone 017687 72263 or visit the website at www.keswick-launch.co.uk

Ullswater Steamers (walks 3, 7, 12 and 14) - **Pooley Bridge** to **Howtown** and **Glenridding**. The first boat from **Pooley Bridge** to **Glenridding** is at 09.45 (winter 12.10) and the last is at 17.05 (winter 16.55). The first boat from **Glenridding** to **Pooley** Bridge is at 10.20 (winter 11.10) and the last is at 16.00 (winter 15.55). Timetables are weather permitting and differ widely according to the time of year. Times given here are only a very rough guide. For full details, phone 017684 82229 or visit the website at www.ullswater-steamers.co.uk

B USEFUL INFORMATION

Tourist Information Centres:

Lake District National Park Information Centre at Ullswater
Beckside Car Park
Glenridding
CA11 0PD
Tel: 017684 82414
Email: ullswatertic@lake-district.gov.uk

Lake District National Park Information Centre at Keswick
Moot Hall
Market Square
Keswick
CA12 5JR
Tel: 017687 72645
Email: keswicktic@lake-district.gov.uk

Cockermouth Tourist Information Centre
Town Hall
Market Street
Cockermouth
CA13 9NP
Tel: 01900 822634

Penrith Tourist Information Centre
Robinson's School
Middlegate
Penrith
Tel: 01768 867466

Accommodation:
For accommodation listings, contact any of the above information centres
or visit one of the many websites dedicated to providing tourist
information for Cumbria. These include www.golakes.co.uk, www.lakes-
online.co.uk, www.lakesnet.co.uk, www.keswick.org,
www.dokeswick.com, www.search-cumbria.com and
www.virtualcumbria.net/accommodation/

Cumbria Tourist Board also runs an accommodation booking line on 0808
1008848. To receive a holiday guide, contact the brochure line on 0870
5133059.

Weather:
For an up-to-date weather forecast for the Lake District, phone 0870
0550575. In the winter, this forecast also includes an assessment of the felltop conditions –including depth, condition and likely locations of snow and
ice – that is updated daily.

Mountain rescue:
To call out a mountain rescue team, dial 999 and ask for mountain rescue.

Fix The Fells:
The Fix the Fells campaign aims to raise £5 million for upland path repairs
in the Lake District. To find out more or to make a donation, visit
www.fixthefells.co.uk

Other outdoor pursuits:
For information on outdoor pursuits such as mountain biking, climbing,
kayaking and para-gliding, visit www.lakedistrictoutdoors.co.uk

Other useful addresses:
The Lake District National Park Authority
Murley Moss
Oxenholme Road
Kendal
Cumbria
LA9 7RL
Tel: 01539 724555
Website: www.lake-district.gov.uk

Cumbria Tourist Board
Ashleigh
Holly Road
Windermere
Cumbria
LA23 2AQ
Tel: 015394 44444
Website: www.golakes.co.uk

National Trust (regional office)
The Hollens
Grasmere
Ambleside
Cumbria
LA22 9QZ
Tel: 0870 609 5391
Website: www.nationaltrust.org.uk

GLOSSARY

arête	a sharp, rocky mountain ridge
baryte	mineral used largely in the manufacture of glass and paint
bothy	a small dwelling, usually temporary, found mostly in upland areas
brock	old English word for badger
cirque	see *corrie*
col	a saddle or pass in the mountains
corrie	a semi-circular mountain recess (or *cirque*) usually formed by glaciation
drumlin	an elongated hill or ridge formed from glacial drift, usually occurring in clusters (drumlin fields)
gowk	Cumberland dialect for cuckoo (and fool)
granophyre	a fine-grained type of granite containing some quartz and feldspar
hause	regional term meaning gap or opening, usually used for a saddle or pass in the mountains
leat	man-made water channel usually leading to a mine or a mill
moraine	sediment deposited by retreating glaciers
tewet	a northern word for the peewit or lapwing

Getting lost is not a pleasant experience, while getting lost in a foreign destination can be distinctly unpleasant. DWG have an excellent reputation for accurately researched and described walking routes, but even we can go further with our revolutionary **Personal Navigator Files**.

All DWG's **Walk!** (colour) and **Walks** (b&w) series of walking guidebooks are researched using modern GPS equipment, giving us an accuracy of better than five metres. GPS gives us extremely accurate walking routes, and DWG knows exactly where our authors have walked. Now we are making this GPS Track and Waypoint information available for GPS users in a Personal Navigator Files CD complete with GPS Utility Special Edition software.

If you have a GPS with a lead to connect it to your PC, then DWG's new **Personal Navigator Files** will mean that you can;
- download Waypoints for our walking routes direct to your gps in seconds.
- download the gps track of a walking route to your gps in seconds.
so that you can follow in the exact footsteps of our walking authors;
now that really is 'vorsprung technik' for walkers.

Personal Navigator Files CD version 3.01 contains :-
- Autorun software explaining PNFs and their use.
- GPS Utility Special Edition software.
- background information for each PNF destination.
- Read Me file for each destination explaining GPS coverage.
- UK GPS Tracks and Waypoints for : **Walk! The Yorkshire Dales** (North & Central)**, Walk! The Peak District** (South)**, Walk! Dartmoor, Walk! The South Pennines, Walk! The South Downs, Walk! The Lake District North, Walk! The Lake District South, Walk! The Brecon Beacons, Walk! Dorset, Walk! Exmoor.**
- Overseas GPS Tracks and Waypoints for: **34 Alpujarras Walks, Sierra de Aracena - a Walk! guidebook, Walk! La Gomera, 35 Madeira Walks, Walk! Mallorca** (North & Mountains)**, Walk! Mallorca** (West)**, 35 Tenerife Walks, Walk! Menorca, Walk! Andorra, Walk! La Palma, Walk! Lanzarote, Walk! Axarquia.**
- Rutland-UK test the accuracy of PNFs on the Hambleton Peninsula.
All of this for just £9.99 from Discovery Walking Guides

 For more information, see DWG websites:-

www.walking.demon.co.uk
and
www.dwgwalking.co.uk

INDEX OF PLACE NAMES